MY MESSAGE IS C.L.E.A.R.

Hope and Strength in the Face of Life's Greatest Adversities

By Gabe Murfitt with Gigi Devine Murfitt

Blessings on your life May the plan be CLEAR

Gigi Murfitt

What People Are Saying About
Gabe Murfitt's Life Message...

One look at my friend Gabe raises *a lot* of questions. Yes, about his physical limitations, but more so, about his smile. Where does this young man get his bright, upbeat attitude? What keeps him going? Answers to these questions and more are what make Gabe's story of faith and courage so riveting. I'm *especially* excited that he is lighting the fire under a whole new generation of young people. So enjoy getting to know Gabe...your outlook on the future will be a lot more *clear!*

—Joni Eareckson Tada
Joni and Friends International Disability Center

I have enjoyed getting to know Gabe. He gives true meaning to the word "perseverance," and he and his strong family have used the platform that Gabe's disability has provided to spread a message of hope and courage. It seems that Gabe has no limits, and his story is one that we can all learn from.

—Cal Ripken, Jr.
Hall of Fame baseball player

Gabe has spent a great deal of time in my fourth-grade classroom. He demonstrates how to thrive in spite of a handicap. His C.L.E.A.R. message really gets students thinking about their own lives, as well as how they treat others. He has practical suggestions on bullying, an area getting great attention in elementary schools. I highly recommend Gabe. Everyone is changed by his presentation.

—Kathy Goodheart
Retired Teacher, Sandstone Elementary School

Gabe captivated the attention of our students in a recent assembly, where he presented his message. Our school has incorporated his C.L.E.A.R. message into our morning meetings. I would invite Gabe back to our school in the future. He had a profound effect on the students, and if I could hire him permanently, I would!

—Stacy Lemelin
Principal, Sandstone Elementary School

Gabe is able to communicate with students of various age groups in an engaging manner. They remember his C.L.E.A.R. message. The kids loved Gabe and would love to have him come back to Valley Christian!

—Gloria Butz
Principal, Valley Christian School

Gabe created a wave of excitement with his dog, Ruth, and his Razor scooter. His C.L.E.A.R. message has been incorporated into the lives of our children, both at school and at home. He profoundly changed one kindergartner forever. Gabe is a hero to the children of McKinley School, as many of them battle homelessness and other trials and tribulations. He has given them HOPE, and they look forward to his arrival each year. His classroom and whole school delivery is stellar, and he invites questions and comments, responding in a very thoughtful and thorough way.

—Pat Lowthian
Fourth-grade teacher, McKinley School

When I hear Gabe Murfitt tell his story, I am mesmerized. This young man is an inspiration to anyone fortunate enough to hear him. Kind, warm, humble, humorous, and insightful—all these things characterize Gabe's presentation.

—Bill Butterworth
Author and speaker

Like a modern-day David, Gabe Murfitt refuses to let his physical stature keep him from confronting his Goliaths head-on. Through the years I have watched this extraordinary young man push against athletic, musical, and academic boundaries to achieve amazing results. I have seen him face the giants of discouragement, disappointment, and loneliness and emerge on the other side with greater confidence, strength, and wisdom. From the moment I met Gabe, I sensed that he and his story would impact many, many lives. This has already happened, and yet, something tells me that he has only begun to influence his generation.

—**Marty Nystrom**
Author, worship leader, and songwriter
Composer of the worship classic "As the Deer"

Gabe's book got my students thinking in a real way that is relevant to their experience, while at the same time, taking them out of any experience that they have been familiar with up to now. Gabe's voice is clearly heard as he shares strategies for dealing with adversity and embracing diversity. Readers are connected to Gabe at the heart and share his roller-coaster ride through adolescence to young adulthood. There are many arenas in education that could benefit from the inclusion of this book in the curriculum. Character education, equity, empathy, and leadership are just a few of the critical child-development issues that have fallen to schools to teach. By sharing his story, Gabe shows students how to "walk the talk," become leaders in their own lives, set goals, and build on their failures as well as their successes. This book is a must for inclusion in the curriculum for any school that aspires to promoting inclusion and a safe school community.

—**Charmaine M. Everett**
English teacher, Fred Moodry Middle School

As a mental health professional, I was drawn to Gabe first by his radiant smile and now by the power and hope offered in these pages. You can learn a great deal about how to reignite a courageous heart, how to walk strong despite circumstances, how to develop a victory attitude. Soak in the powerful lessons in these pages. It's a page-turner and life-changer. There is Hope.

—Gregory L. Jantz,
PhD, C.E.D.S.
Founder of The Center - "A Place of Hope"

Gabe Murfitt is a rare and exceptionally inspiring person. I am certain that anyone who reads his story will be encouraged by the incredibly positive outlook he has on life and living with his particular physical disability. He challenges me personally to see opportunities amidst trials and to trust God who is far greater than what we might see as limitations. This young man is a hero with a powerful message of hope.

—Jana Alayra
Singer/songwriter, speaker

MY MESSAGE IS C.L.E.A.R.

Hope and Strength in the Face of Life's Greatest Adversities

By Gabe Murfitt with Gigi Devine Murfitt

GABRIEL'S FOUNDATION OF HOPE
Bringing HOPE to the world

ISBN 13: 978-0-9850932-1-1
ISBN 10: 0-9850-9321-8

Cover Photo: Yuen Lui Studios
Cover Design: Bob Horn, Eternal Design Graphics

CONTENTS

ACKNOWLEDGMENTS

From Gabe

FIRST, I'D LIKE to thank God for doing all that He has done in my life and for making this book possible.

To you, my reader, thank you for taking time to read this book; I am so happy that you're reading it. I wish I could say I wrote the whole thing, but that isn't true. I'm grateful for my mom, who worked hard to help me get my stories on paper. So even though these are my stories, it is really her book.

I'm thankful to my parents, who continue to show me how to live life with a positive attitude. From the moment I was born, they have loved me unconditionally and don't treat me any differently than they treat my older brother, Zane. I'm grateful for the encouragement they have given me all these years.

I grew up with a very supportive big brother, and I'm thankful for the way Zane has helped me to be successful. We have had great times sharing life together. He has been my mentor and friend.

I can't wait for you to read my stories in this book. I hope they encourage you to live with a C.L.E.A.R. vision for your life.

From Gigi

This book would not be possible without the support and encouragement of my husband, Steve. He has walked alongside me in this journey of raising our boys, Zane and Gabe. We've traveled into unknown territories together and made the best of every new turn in the road.

Now that our sons are adults, Steve and I get to spend the rest of our lives continuing to become all God has called us to be. I look forward to our story unfolding as we grow old together with a song in our hearts.

To my firstborn, Zane, I have loved you from the moment I found out I was pregnant. I hoped and prayed for a boy who would make his mom proud. And you have done above and beyond that. Not only have you lived a life worthy of praise, but also now you've given us a beautiful daughter-in-law in your wife, Kelsey. We are excited to watch where God will take you. I have a feeling that it will continue to be an exciting time.

To Gabe, your smile warmed my heart within moments after your birth. I continue to be amazed as your story unfolds. I still can't believe that God picked me to be your mom. Thank you for allowing me to write this book with you. You have given me much to write about. I'm really proud of you.

We have a large extended family to thank for the way they have helped mold our two sons into well-loved young men. Thank you to the Murfitt and Devine families. You are truly a testimony of the "it takes a village to raise a child" theory.

I believe with all of my being that Gabe's amazing story would not be what it is without the love and support from our community of faith. We had friends, including the Sabandals, Furnstahls, Eickoffs, and several other families in our first home-group who prayed and helped us navigate through life. The people in our current fellowship group, which is led by Marlene and Bill Brubaker, are like family. Their prayers and encouragement keep us going when we hit a few bumps in the road.

So many good friends have helped us be better parents along the way. I especially want to thank Karen Bartsch, who has been able to point us to healing in some of the difficult struggles of life. Karen, I truly believe you are heaven-sent and a testimony that many people have a divine purpose. I am so glad to be a part of what God has called you to do. Your honesty in the hard things has made us grow to be more like God meant for us to be.

My good friend Cheryl Penn has helped us document Gabe's story by interviewing him on video. She continues to ask great questions that bring out the best of each story. When my schedule was frustrating and I was unable to write, she encouraged me to know that God's timing is perfect. She reminded me to trust that everything would all come together. Thanks, Cheryl. I appreciate your friendship more than you know.

Our first readers, Kathy Goodheart, Cheryl Penn, Marty Nystrom, Meghan Bailey, Lynn Burgher, Jim Devine, Karen Bartsch, and Judy Devine helped make the stories flow. Thank you for taking the time to give us your feedback on the manuscript.

A group of Fred Moodry Middle School students took on a school project to review this book. Thank you to these helpful students and their teacher, Charmaine Everett, who helped facilitate this review. We appreciate your valuable feedback.

I am grateful for our coaching editor, Barbara Kois. It has been fun to share the process with you. We've even shed a few tears as moms who want the best for our children. Your encouraging phone calls have blessed me. Thank you for your help.

I've enjoyed the last several years as Gabe has developed his life story into the C.L.E.A.R. message we share in this book. There are precious moments in the car in between school assemblies when he throws a new idea into his speech. Each time, I am in awe of the way his young mind put the ideas together.

As Gabe continues to speak to crowds young and old, I'm sure

ACKNOWLEDGMENTS

he'll surprise us with new stories and ideas to help us learn how to live successful lives. I'm excited to share this message that has been on Gabe's heart for many years.

INTRODUCTION (GABE)

SO, WHAT MAKES my story so special? My story really isn't that different from yours, except maybe that I get to tell it in a book. And I share it to encourage you to live life to your greatest potential.

Sure, I was born with a unique body. But if you think about it, you have a unique design too. It just so happens that my design is also a little on the unusual side. My arms are short, and my legs are crooked, but for the most part, I'm more like you than I am different.

Although I have faced some challenges, I have found hope and strength in the face of great adversity. I enjoy sharing my strategies with people who are just like you. I figure that when you find something that works for you, it is a good idea to pass it on and help someone else.

There are many things in my life that have helped me to work through these challenges. To make it simple, I took the letters in the word "clear" and created an acrostic (C.L.E.A.R.) with a message that helps explain the five things I focus on as I strive to live a successful life. My message is C.L.E.A.R. to me, and I hope to make it C.L.E.A.R. to you.

The "C" is for *Courage*. It takes great courage to live in a body that's different. On some days it takes courage just to get up and face the world. I will help you find the courage to face your everyday challenges.

INTRODUCTION

The "L" is for *Leadership*. Everyone is a leader in one way or another. As a leader, I am encouraging and compassionate. I will give you some tools to help you be an awesome leader in your school, work place, and/or family.

The "E" is for *Endurance*. Endurance is the ability to last. There are many things in our lives we must endure to get through each day. You'll learn how to endure whatever it is you are going through, even the really hard things.

The "A" is for *Attitude*. Of all the letters in the word C.L.E.A.R., this is one of the most important. I think a positive attitude is necessary to achieve great things. You may look at my body and wonder how I get through life. Yes, it's hard to live with short arms and crooked legs, but it is possible when you choose to keep a positive attitude.

The "R" stands for *Respect*. Respecting yourself is the most important thing you can do to live a successful life. Respecting others will help you to achieve the goals you desire. After reading the stories in this book, you will have a list of people I respect. They have helped me to be everything I am called to be.

I can't wait to share the stories and give you hope for a C.L.E.A.R. future. So let's get on with it.

CHAPTER 1

MY BODY

LET'S GET THIS issue out of the way right off the bat. We'll talk about my uniquely formed body. Most people who see me for the first time are very curious. Some people point. Some stare. I've even seen a few small kids cry because they've never seen someone like me.

Once, the producer for *The Oprah Winfrey Show* asked me if I had a message to send to people who point and stare at me. I told her, "Don't judge a book by its cover. I might look different, but I'm actually not that different."

I like it best when people take the time to approach me with a "hello." Something as simple as that breaks the barrier of fear, and before long, we have lots to talk about. It's right about then that most people realize we are more alike than we are different.

I wish I could tell you why I look like this, but we just don't know. It's simply the way I developed before I was born. I have arms that are about three inches long. My legs are bent at the knee and stuck that way. (Think about how you sit "criss-cross applesauce," and that's how my legs are fused.) My ear canals are closed because there is bone covering up the holes. That is why I wear a hearing aid.

After I was born, the doctors at Seattle Children's Hospital tried to figure out what to call my birth defects. They told us it's probably caused by a mismatch of my parents' genes. It's all pretty complicated,

1

and my parents never did a full test to find out. We figure that it doesn't really matter if we know why I'm like this. I just try to focus on what I can do with what I have, not on what is missing in my body or why it happened.

The doctors had never seen anybody exactly like me. But guess what? They've never seen anybody exactly like you either. We are all unique. We each have our own DNA. I'm a little different. You're a little different in your own way. Rather than measure our differences, I hope we can just accept that every person is unique in his or her design.

In the days after I was born, the doctors ran a bunch of tests, like x-rays, CT scans, and blood work. Even after all those tests, they couldn't figure out exactly what to call my syndrome, so they made up the name. Get ready for this, because it's a couple of big words: *Pseudo-Thalidomide TetraPhocomelia* (pronounced: soo-doh-thuh-lid-uh-mahyd te-truh foh-koh-mee-lee-uh). Whew! I hope you never get that word on a spelling test.

I suggest you Google *Pseudo-Thalidomide TetraPhocomelia* and read all of the interesting things about it. The *Pseudo-Thalidomide* part of the word means that I look like people whose mom took the drug Thalidomide while they were pregnant. This happened in the 1960s and caused babies to be born with limb deficiencies. This drug was later banned for women who are pregnant.

My mom didn't take any medicine while she was pregnant. So to help explain in the medical records what I look like, they use the word "pseudo," which means "not authentic in spite of appearances." Although I appear to be like a Thalidomide-affected patient, my birth defects were not caused by Thalidomide.

Basically, this big set of words means that the bones in my arms and legs didn't grow correctly while I was developing in my mom's womb. The easiest way for me to explain it is to have you stretch your right arm out in front of you. Go ahead and try it. First touch your elbow. Now touch your wrist. There are two bones between your elbow and wrist called the radius and ulna bones. Those bones never grew in my arms. The bone that did develop is the one that goes from the elbow up to the shoulder. It is called the humerus bone, and mine is only a few inches long. When you look at me, it looks like my hands come out of my shoulders. I also don't have thumbs, and my fingers are stiff. I can only bend the knuckles on my pointer fingers. But I can use my hands to feed myself, type, and write. I also play a mean set of drums.

Let's talk about my legs. When my legs were forming, the bones at my knee joint jumbled all together as one bone. They are bent and fused (which means they are stuck) at about a 45° angle. No matter how hard I try, I can't straighten them. When I move my leg, the movement comes from my hip and ankle joints.

In order for me to get around, I scoot on my butt or walk by putting my right foot and left knee on the ground. You should try it. It's not that easy, but I actually get around pretty well. It is all part of figuring out how to live with what you've got.

When I was a baby, my mom propped me up inside of a foam square. It was a foot tall and about four feet wide. It had a hole cut in the center. One of the occupational therapists at Children's Hospital came up with the idea. When I sat inside the hole, it kept me from tipping over. I could reach the toys she put on the foam. I loved it when she gave me M&M® candy or Cheerios®. I could pinch them between my pointer and middle fingers and pop them into my mouth. Sitting in this foam contraption made my stomach muscles strong. To this day I have a tight "six-pack" stomach because I use my stomach muscles for balance and to help me get up from a lying-down position.

Because the canals on my ears are closed over with bone, I can't hear like you do. Here's how you can better understand my hearing issues. Plug your ears with your pointer fingers. You'll notice that the sound isn't very clear because your fingers block it from entering your ear. For me, it is skull bone that stops the sound from clearly reaching my inner ear.

When I was five years old, I had surgery to drill through my skull to open the hole into my left inner ear. But scar tissue covered the hole, and the surgery didn't work. So my hearing aid has an oscillator on one side that vibrates my skull and a microphone on the other side of my head that magnifies the sound. My eardrum catches the vibration so I can hear almost 100 percent. It works pretty well, but sometimes it picks up weird vibration sounds like buzzing lights or tires rolling on the streets.

The hearing aid stays on my head with a headband. One time a guy asked me what I was listening to when he noticed that I wear a headset. I replied, "This is actually a bone conductive hearing aid. So I'm listening to you."

If I'm not wearing my hearing aid, I can still hear enough of what you are saying to understand. Plus I taught myself to read lips. I watch your mouth form the words, which helps me to figure out what I can't hear.

By the time this book goes to press, I will have had surgery to implant a new kind of hearing device into my skull. It is called the BAHA® (Bone Anchored Hearing Aid). I am so excited because it will help me to hear much better. I will write about it on our website so that you can follow the progress of this new technology. (See http://www.GabesHOPE.org.)

You're probably wondering how I perform basic tasks with such an unusual body. I'd like to address the most common questions people ask. I actually am able to do most of my daily tasks just like you, only slightly differently. For instance, I have to stand on a stool to reach the sink when I brush my teeth. I can squeeze the toothpaste onto my toothbrush, but it's easier to get help so I don't squirt toothpaste all over the counter.

I can take a shower on my own. My parents have a shower head that lowers down to my level. We also have lower nozzles that I'm able to reach to turn the water on and off. I use a long scrub brush to help me reach my head.

I have never worn a pair of jeans. We buy elastic-band sweat pants because they're easier to get on over my bent knees. It has taken a lot of practice to figure out how to dress myself. I can even put socks on my feet by using the big toe on the opposite foot to pull them on. Each year I figure out some new tool to make dressing an easier process.

When I eat, I use utensils just like you. Since my thumbs don't work, I hold my fork between my pointer finger and my middle finger on my left hand. I don't have a lot of strength in my right hand, so I need help if my food needs to be cut up. If I'm drinking out of a plastic cup, I can bite the cup with my teeth and tip it to allow the liquid to pour into my mouth. But it's much easier to use a straw. My favorite foods you ask? Beef stroganoff would be my first choice and pepperoni pizza my second.

I like to experiment with ways to do the things my friends do. I even figured out how to hold a game controller for Xbox by balancing it on my right foot and holding it steady between my hands. I grab the joystick between my pointer and middle fingers and press the buttons with my knuckles. I like to play sports games like football, basketball, and soccer.

When my parents bought me the Xbox Kinect, I had to get creative in order to play. Kinect uses a motion sensor to track your entire body when you play. My arms are so short that the sensor didn't see them. I tried using my drumsticks as arms, but they weren't thick enough to be recognized by the sensor. After that, I improvised and put gloves on the lint rollers we use to remove dog hair from my pants. I look pretty funny holding two lint rollers with gloves flopping around as I play the games. But it works.

When I was a baby, no one taught me how to scoot or roll across the room. I was determined to get to my blanket and/or toys, so I figured out how to get to them. If my mom laid me on the floor to drink a bottle, she propped it under a pillow. One day she found me holding my bottle between my feet. I had moved my knees close to my chest and put the bottle back in my mouth, holding it tightly between my feet. Trust me; when you're determined to find a means to do the things you really want to do, you will figure out a way. Just keep trying.

People often ask me this question: "When did you first realize you had birth defects?" I can actually remember the moment I realized the truth. It sits in my mind as if it happened just this morning.

I didn't see myself as "different" or "disabled" until I was in kindergarten. My mom pulled into the parking lot at school. There were hundreds of kids running around on the playground, having a good time before school started. Zane got out of the van and ran to play with his friends.

As Mom was getting my wheelchair out, I said, "I don't want to take my wheelchair to school today."

Mom replied, "Sweetheart, you have to take your wheelchair. It is supposed to rain today. You can't scoot on your bottom because the ground will be wet. You'll get your pants muddy."

"I want to run onto the playground like Zane. Why do I have to use a wheelchair?"

"You'll *always* have a wheelchair, Gabe. It's the way you get around."

"What? You mean when I'm in third grade like Zane, I won't have long legs and be able to run like him? Are my arms going to grow long like his?"

MY MESSAGE IS C.L.E.A.R.

Mom turned and looked at me. "No, Gabe, you are missing bones in your arms. They aren't going to grow. The bones in your legs are fused together. I'm sorry, Honey; unless God gives us a miracle, they won't grow long like Zane's."

A lump formed in my throat. I couldn't believe what my mom said. I really thought I would be just like Zane. I honestly imagined that my arms and legs would grow so I could ride a bike. I could see myself running out on the playground with everyone else. The whole thing made me stinking sad. I didn't want to cry, but I couldn't help it. The tears burned in my eyes. I blinked and looked at the kids running out on the playground. They were blurry through the tears.

Mom reached over and hugged me. She started crying too. We sat in the van for a long time. Neither of us said a word. Then Mom spoke in a crackly voice. "Sweetheart, I want more than anything for you to have long arms and long legs just like Zane. I don't understand why God allowed you to be like this. We can't dwell on that. But I do know He made you precious and handsome and awesome. I want you to see yourself as someone who is set apart to change lives, rather than focusing on the fact that you are disabled. I know God plans to use you for mighty things. We just have to trust that He will help us find a way to help you do the things you want to do."

She rubbed my hair. "I believe God is a healer, Gabe. Maybe someday He will give you those missing bones. But in the meantime, I want to help you trust God. We will pray and ask Him how we make it to the next step. He sees your life from a higher place, and He can direct your path to the good things that will happen. I just know it."

I looked at my mom. "Thanks, Mom. I don't want to talk about it anymore. Will you get my wheelchair out of the van, please? I don't want to be late for class."

We talked through my feelings about my disability over the next several months. Before long, I decided that I would make the best of the body God gave me. It wasn't like this better attitude happened overnight, though. It was a process of working out my feelings. My family shared many more tearful moments over the years.

I had to come to grips with the idea that God allowed my disability. I wrestled with the question, "Why me, God?" My parents wondered if they had done something wrong. Praying and talking to wise counselors helped us walk through our questions. We all had to process our thoughts in our own ways. There were some days when I was depressed. There were other days when disappointment reigned in my heart, like the time I cried with Zane when I realized that playing soccer was too dangerous for me.

Zane was playing soccer on a team with his friends. At the end of the season, we had a party at the indoor soccer field. We decided to have the parents play against the kids in a scrimmage match. I begged mom to let me play. She thought it was too dangerous, but I convinced her I could handle it.

It was so fun being out on the field with Zane's friends and their siblings. We kicked the ball around for awhile to warm up. I felt like part of the team when I passed the ball off to Zane and he scored. I did my happy dance. It was awesome.

I was having a blast running up and down the field until Zane's coach kicked the ball hard. It soared through the air and came right to me like a heat-seeking missile. It hit my head, and I went down fast. *Ouch! That hurt.* Then I almost got kicked in the kidney. After that, mom and dad were convinced there would be no more soccer for me. There was no way they would risk my being seriously hurt. I knew they were right, but I was bummed.

Zane told me if he could give me his arms and legs for a soccer season, he would, just so I could experience it. We laughed about how good I'd be with his body and my toughness.

Accepting my body has been a day-by-day process. I am grateful that my family helped me learn to live in the skin I'm in. It sure beats trying to be somebody I was never meant to be. Too many kids these days try to change into somebody other than the amazing person God created them to be. He created every single person as a unique treasure.

When I start to get down about my body, I remind myself of what God says about me in Scripture:

> For you created my inmost being; you knit me together in my mother's womb. I praise you because I am fearfully and wonderfully made; your works are wonderful, I know that full well. My frame was not hidden from you when I was made in the secret place, when I was woven together in the depths of the earth. Your eyes saw my unformed body; all the days ordained for me were written in your book before one of them came to be. How precious to me are your thoughts, God! How vast is the sum of them! Were I to count them, they would outnumber the grains of sand—when I awake, I am still with you.
>
> —Psalm 139:13–18

The Bible also reminds me that there is a plan for me and it is good:

> "For I know the plans I have for you," declares the LORD, "plans to prosper you and not to harm you, plans to give you hope and a future."
>
> —Jeremiah 29:11

I like how the Bible says that God saw me even before I was born. He isn't surprised that I came out with short arms and deformed legs. He doesn't call me "disabled" or "different." He uses words like "wonderful" and "precious."

God likes every part of me. He likes every part of you too. He created you for this day and this hour because he knew the world would need someone like you. God is excited to watch you change the world. I really hope you realize that truth.

My mom told me that God even knows the number of hairs on

my head. I think that's unbelievable because I have a lot of hair. I wonder how He counted them when my dad shaved me nearly bald one hot summer day when I asked him to give me a buzz cut. Thankfully, my hair grows fast. Even that small detail about my hair is important to God.

Do you understand how precious you are? Take a good look at the verses I quoted from Psalm 139. God's thoughts about you are more than all the grains of sand on all the beaches in the world. God thinks about you a whole lot! God also has a plan and a purpose for everything about you. He gave you gifts and talents that He wants you to use. He loves you more than you could ever know. That fact has helped me to live in this really different body. I know God will help me live every day. I hope this reality will help you too.

If you struggle with believing the truth about how much God loves you, I hope you will talk to a pastor or counselor or friend who can help you. Contact us at Gabriel's Foundation of HOPE if you need to be encouraged. There is contact information in the resource section at the end of this book.

So, now that we got the facts about my anatomy out of the way, let's talk about something more interesting. I'm blessed to have a pretty awesome family, so let me tell you a little bit about them.

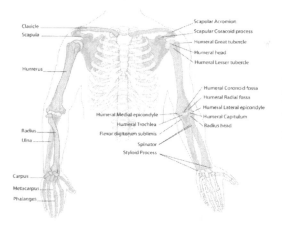

I am missing the radius and ulna bones in my arms. My humerus bone is only about three inches long. I am missing my thumb bones too.

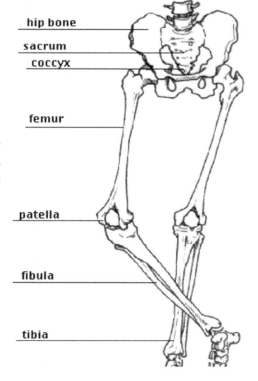

My femur is fused at the knee (patella) to my tibia and fibula in a bent position. I can't straighten my legs.

11

CHAPTER 2

MY FAMILY

MY MOM AND DAD are amazing people. You might be thinking I said that because my mom helped me write this book, but I'm not kidding. They have helped me learn to live a full life even though I was born with a body that doesn't work like most bodies. "You have to make the best of what you've got." That's what they've always told me. And so far, that strategy has worked for me.

My dad, Steve, grew up in Phillipsburg, Montana. He played football and basketball in high school and college. We have a great time going to games and talking sports with each other. He has two brothers and two sisters. His parents, my grandma Barbara and grandpa Zane Murfitt, welcomed me with love and a smile. They have really helped to make my life better.

Before my grandma Barbara died, she was my brilliant seamstress. Most shirts don't fit me right off the racks at stores because the sleeves cover my hands, and Grandma Barbara was a wizard on the sewing machine. She adjusted my shirts and made them the perfect size for my short arms. Every few months she sent me a few more shirts. She was amazing, and I miss her.

Grandpa Zane and I also talk about sports. He checks in on me each week, and I enjoy spending time with him when we go to

MY FAMILY

Montana. I'm blessed with a really nice grandpa who supports me in all of my activities.

I have eight first cousins and a big extended family on the Murfitt side. We have a good time when our families get together. Now some of my cousins are having babies, so our family is always growing.

I have an army of cousins on my mom's side of the family. She is the eighth of ten kids raised in Anaconda, Montana, which is about thirty miles from where my dad grew up. With all my aunts and uncles and cousins, we have over sixty-five people on that side of the family. It can get pretty crazy when we get together.

I never knew my grandpa Bob Devine. He died when my mom was a little girl. But I loved my grandma Helen. She had to overcome a lot in high school because she broke her back in an accident. Grandma Helen was paralyzed for over six months, but she fought hard to get better and eventually walked again. She could relate to my challenges because she limped and had to walk with a cane. Grandma Helen helped me understand how to deal with people staring at us when we were out in public together. She dealt with this issue most of her life.

I miss my two grandmas. They were great ladies. But I know I'll get to see them in heaven. I'm glad they knew Jesus.

Zane is three years older than I am. From the day I was born, he has taken good care of me. When we were little, we played football together. I wore a Dallas Cowboys helmet, and he wore a Philadelphia Eagles helmet. He played on his knees so we'd be about the same height. It's a good thing we wore helmets and shoulder pads, because we hit each other hard.

I loved playing catch with Zane in our yard when we were kids. He showed me how to dribble a basketball and kick the soccer ball around. I learned a lot about sports from playing with him, and when I sat on the sidelines to watch him play. I appreciate that he always took time to show me new things.

MY MESSAGE IS C.L.E.A.R.

My sister-in-law is Kelsey. She's been a good friend since I was in elementary school. We get along great, and I'm glad she joined our family in the summer of 2009.

I won't hold it against Zane and Kelsey since they graduated from Washington State University, but I definitely prefer the University of Washington Huskies. Go Dawgs! We have a fun sibling rivalry, but it drives my mom crazy when our college teams play each other and we give each other grief.

The support of my family has been a huge part of my life. Like my mom always says, "When they say it takes a village to raise kids these days, I don't have to go outside my family tree to experience the village." But we do also have some really good friends from our neighborhood and our church family who have contributed to my life by encouraging me and supporting me in my activities.

If you don't have a supportive family, don't lose heart. God is invested in a positive outcome in your life. He comes to the aid of lonely people like you and like me. He looks after the fatherless and the widowed. He plants organizations and churches in neighborhoods to bring us the support we need. Here is another verse in the Bible that reminds me of this truth:

> Sing to God, sing in praise of his name, extol him who rides on the clouds; rejoice before him—his name is the LORD. A father to the fatherless, a defender of widows, is God in his holy dwelling. God sets the lonely in families, he leads out the prisoners with singing; but the rebellious live in a sun-scorched land.
> —Psalm 68:4–6

I meet once a week with my small group at The City Church. We meet to pray and encourage each other to work towards our goals. We challenge one another to use our God-given strengths and talents to live life to the best of our abilities.

MY FAMILY

I hope you will take time to check into a church in your area or a youth organization where you can get plugged into a supportive group of people. You're worth it.

My family (L to R): My CCI dog, Ruth, and our family dog, Donovan, lounge in front of my family. Behind the dogs (L to R) are my brother, Zane; me; my sister-in-law, Kelsey; my mom, Gigi; and my dad, Steve.
(Photo taken by Yuen Lui and used by permission.)

CHAPTER 3

MY MOBILITY—HOW I GET AROUND

I STARTED DRIVING when I was two years old. My first wheels came on a bright blue wheelchair with the brand name Turbo Bobcat painted on the side. It had an elevator in the seat to lower me to the ground so I could hop off and play on the floor. I used a cool little joystick in my left hand to drive. It's the same kind of joystick that you use with video games.

Often other kids wanted to ride on my wheelchair. I would give them the following instruction: "Hang on because I'm going fast!" There was a flat space on the back where they could sit or kneel, but they needed to hold on. I think I dumped only one friend off the back because he didn't follow my instruction. The next time I gave him a ride, he hung on for dear life. He was a smart kid.

Because I was so young when I got this wheelchair, I don't remember the details surrounding it. But my mom and dad like to tell the story of how God provided a way for us to buy that $18,000 chair. Yes, you read that right; it cost $18,000 for a motorized wheelchair.

My dad's insurance company had refused to insure me. Mom's insurance didn't think I needed a power wheelchair, so they didn't want to pay for it. So our friend Diane Newman-Holmstrom spread the word about our situation.

MY MOBILITY—HOW I GET AROUND

Family, friends, and a few strangers raised money and donated it to a special-needs trust fund. The cost of setting up this trust was donated by a lawyer. My mom's co-workers established a bank account and challenged fellow employees to help raise money for my chair.

My grandma Helen organized a raffle, and people donated items like homemade quilts and gift certificates from businesses in the area. My aunt Judy pulled together a group of people and raised money with a mouse race. My mom's co-workers had a computer bashing party, where money was donated for a chance to hit an old computer with a sledge hammer. Some of the customer service employees enjoyed taking their frustrations out on the computers that had been giving them headaches. Each activity was organized so I could get my wheelchair.

We still don't know the names of some of the people who gave money to the fund. But because of the donations, my mom and dad were able to pay the balance of the wheelchair costs and purchase a used van to transport it. If you are one of those donors, I want to send you a big thank-you hug. Your gift gave me mobility and freedom. It helped me to gain independence and confidence.

I learned at this young age that what seems to be impossible is possible when people pray, asking God to provide for their needs. God used people's kind hearts and generous wallets to help me get my wheelchair and van. And I don't doubt that He will do it again.

When I was ten years old, I outgrew my first wheelchair. My next chair was fire engine red. It had the same elevator seat and a cool horn and headlights. I was thankful that this time my mom and dad's insurance helped pay more of the cost. I think that my red wheelchair was my favorite, but after five years, I outgrew it.

Now I drive a bigger chair that has a different kind of elevator on the front. This one is the fastest of them all, but it's not as sleek. I drive with my right foot, using the same kind of joystick as the one I used with my hand. I'm grateful for these wheels; they help me get to where I need to go.

One of my favorite modes of transportation is a Razor® scooter. I put my left knee on the skateboard and push off the ground with my right foot. Because the scooter is adjustable, I can keep the handle on the shortest setting so that my hands can rest at the perfect height.

I was in the fifth grade when I got my first scooter. I was on that thing from dawn until dusk on Saturdays and summer days. My mom had to buy boxes of Band-Aids because I kept scraping my knee on the asphalt when I cruised with my friends in our cul-de-sac. That was a very fun summer because I loved hanging out with friends.

Now my biggest prayer is for a different kind of mobility. I would like to drive a car. Well, really, I'd like to drive my own Chevy Corvette. Someday I will invent a way for my wheelchair to fit into such a hot sports car. When it comes to dreaming about my Corvette, I always say, "Never say never."

I know I will be able to drive a vehicle because I've done it before. When I turned sixteen, I went to a driving program at the University of Washington. After a woman named Frances measured my arms and legs and did some strength tests on me, she was ready to show me that I could drive.

We loaded my wheelchair into a huge University of Washington van. I had the option of parking my wheelchair in the space where the driver's seat usually sits, since they could remove the seat and lock my wheelchair in place, but I didn't want to remove the driver's seat. I liked the captain's chair that swiveled to let me hop from my wheelchair onto the seat. We tied down my wheelchair in the center of the van so it wouldn't move, and then I jumped in the captain's chair and buckled the seatbelt. This option felt more normal, and Frances agreed it was best.

My heart was pounding with excitement. Frances opened up a box of tools and went to work. She attached a small steering wheel near the driver's side window, putting it in just the right place for me to reach it with my short left arm. It had a ball to hold on to so I could turn the van. Then Frances brought the pedals closer to my legs. She attached a long extension rod and a square block to the regular pedals, which allowed me to push left for the gas and right for the brake. Finally, she showed me the buttons on a fancy computer that was within reach of my right hand. With this computer, I started the engine, used the blinkers and lights, and turned on the windshield wipers. It also had controls for the windows, doors, air-conditioning, and radio.

After some instruction, Frances asked, "Are you ready for this, Gabe?"

"Let's do it!" I pressed the button to start the van and a different button to put the van in drive. Then I pulled out of the parking lot. I couldn't believe I was driving a van.

My parents were relieved to know that Frances had control of everything from the passenger side. That way, she could take over if things got a little hairy. Even so, Mom and Dad sat in the back of the van praying. I think my mom squeezed my dad's hand until his knuckles were purple. I thought it was funny looking at their scared faces in the rearview mirror. It was the first time I had ever driven a car. Who wouldn't be scared?

But everybody forgot that I had been driving since I was two years old. It was a piece of cake. I took to it like a duck to the water. It all felt natural to me.

I drove around Magnuson Park for over an hour. I turned corners. I parked. I made a U-turn. And the good news is, I did all of this without hitting parked cars. There were a few scary moments when everyone leaned to the right, hoping I'd move back over the center line. Then they'd lean to the left when I swerved a little close to the parked cars. Frances and my parents were relieved that I missed the other cars every time. I was pretty proud.

MY MESSAGE IS C.L.E.A.R.

It was so exciting to think of the possibility of driving myself to school or to a movie or over to a friend's house, but then we got the bad news about the price. About two weeks after my trial drive, we got the quote with the cost of a wheelchair accessible van and the required driving modification equipment. It was over $100,000! I couldn't believe it! In some towns, that amount of money could buy a nice house.

I was really disappointed; I knew we didn't have that kind of money. But I'm not giving up on getting my van because I know that God will provide wheels for me once again. Sometimes we have to wait to get the things we need or want. So I wait patiently. I just know I'll get that vehicle someday.

In the meantime, my parents drive me where I need to go, or I take the Metro bus.

I realize that having mobility issues can be very difficult. You may be going through your own challenges with getting where you need to go. Maybe your body doesn't work like you wish it would, and now you have to walk with a cane or ride in a wheelchair. My mom's cousin Ken had both legs amputated, and he has to deal with two prosthetic legs. Or perhaps you can't afford a decent car. I know firsthand it can be hard, and I understand that we all face different issues. But please don't give up hope. I encourage you to keep pursuing a solution to your mobility or access issues. I am confident you will find an answer that will make your life better.

MY MOBILITY—HOW I GET AROUND

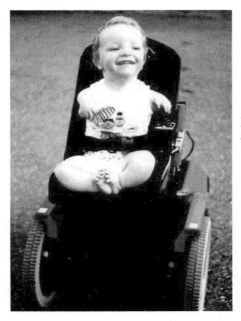

My first wheelchair at age two—Turbo Bobcat.

Here I am smelling the tulips in my Permobil® wheelchair complete with headlights and a horn. This hot red machine was my favorite wheelchair.

MY MESSAGE IS C.L.E.A.R.

This is my Invacare® Arrow Storm Series wheelchair. Ruth is helping me turn the lights on.

I ride my Razor® scooter for exercise.

CHAPTER 4

MY BEST FRIEND

IHAVE A new best friend. Her name is Ruth. She is beautiful. She has dark-black hair and big, brown eyes. She has hung out with me every day since we first met in August 2009. At first, I wasn't sure if she was the one for me. But after spending only a day and a half with her, we both knew we were a match made in heaven.

The best thing about Ruth is that she is a social butterfly. Sometimes I can be shy when I'm in a new setting, but Ruth helps break the ice. I think it is rather funny that people are more comfortable interacting with her than they are with me. But that's the way it is.

I have been joking with my friends that ever since I got Ruth as my companion, she's like a chick magnet. After all, what girl doesn't want to pet a beautiful dog?

Yes, my best friend, Ruth, is a dog. She is one-quarter Golden Retriever and three-quarters black Labrador retriever. This amazing dog was given to me as a gift from the nonprofit organization called Canine Companions for Independence® (CCI). Check out their website, http://www.CCI.org, to learn more about the wonderful things they have been doing since 1975 to help people with disabilities.

Danny and Lisa Akin are volunteer puppy raisers for CCI. They trained Ruth from the time she was eight weeks old until she was about eighteen months old. Then she went to the Santa Rosa,

California, training facility for more intense training. I am so grateful for all of the trainers that helped Ruth become the dog she is today. They did such a wonderful job with her.

The process of receiving a dog from CCI can take up to two years, but no matter how long the process takes, it is well worth it. I filled out the application in the fall of 2008 and expected to wait until 2010 for them to decide if I could get a dog. But God really blessed me with a shorter wait.

My dad, brother and I were out getting fitted for our tuxedos on June 11, 2009, which was the day before Zane's wedding. I got a call from CCI, informing me that my application had been accepted. They told me I was invited to go through team training later that summer. I did my happy dance.

The timing of my getting Ruth was totally orchestrated by God. I was really struggling with the fact that my brother was getting married and moving five hours away. I love my sister-in-law, Kelsey, and I was really excited to have her join our family, but I was saddened by the realization that the times I spent hanging out with Zane were going to change. I envisioned a really lonely summer.

My parents had been praying all along that I would find some good friends. My counselor, Karen, helped me turn my attention from feeling sorry for myself toward focusing on God's good and perfect plan for my future. I really saw that God knew exactly what I was going through when I received Ruth right after Zane and Kelsey moved. God is like that. He provides for my needs in His perfect timing, and that makes me smile.

In August 2009, I spent two weeks in the Santa Rosa training facility learning the fifty commands Ruth knows. We stayed in the dorms on the CCI campus with other families who were there receiving dogs at the same time. Not only did I leave California with a new canine service dog, but also I left with a new group of lifelong friends.

MY MESSAGE IS C.L.E.A.R.

Life can be very lonely sometimes. With Ruth as my helpful companion, the days are not so lonely anymore. She's willing to do just about anything to help make my life easier. And she doesn't seem to mind. She is a wonderful addition to my life.

Sometimes I can't reach the door handle, so she will open the door for me. One time I got stuck on an elevator because I couldn't reach the button. That was kind of scary. But now Ruth presses the buttons for me. If I'm not in my wheelchair, I stand about three feet tall. So unless I have a stick to help me reach, I can't even turn on the lights in our kitchen. So I just ask Ruth, and she turns them on for me. She makes it look so easy.

Another practical thing Ruth does for me is she helps me take my socks off. The command I use is the word "tug." She gently grabs the toe of my sock with her teeth. Then she backs up, tugging the sock off my foot. Once it's off, she gives it to me.

One time I was demonstrating how Ruth tugs my socks off at a school assembly. The floor was slippery, and my socks were on tight. She dragged me halfway across the gym floor. The students erupted in laughter, but it didn't stop Ruth from completing her job.

Ruth enjoys coming to college with me. My Ruth is smart. I wouldn't be surprised if she earns an honorary college degree someday. She is sort of a combination of a valedictorian and a cheerleader. She is smart and full of personality.

I'm often asked how Ruth helps in class. If I drop my pencil, she picks it up. The doors and elevator buttons become a job for her too. When she's not helping me, she lies under my desk and sleeps through most of my classes. On some days, I want to crawl on the floor and snuggle right up with her. She causes some snickers sometimes when she dreams during class and starts moving her legs as if she is running. She even snored one time during a quiet part of the lecture. How can you blame her? I have had a few professors almost put me to sleep too.

MY BEST FRIEND

I'll never spend another Friday night alone because of Ruth. She is an example of the way God has provided for me during the lonely days. I hope you get to meet her someday.

So far you've learned about my unusual body, and you know a little about how I get around. You've also met my family and my dog. Now I'll share the message that has helped me live a successful life. This message is C.L.E.A.R. to me, so let me make it C.L.E.A.R. to you.

Me and my best friend, Ruth, on the day I graduated from the CCI training.

CHAPTER 5

MY C.L.E.A.R. MESSAGE

I STARTED SPEAKING at schools when I was in the seventh grade. Zane and I were part of a nonprofit organization called Positive Programs, Inc. Shari Rusch Furnstahl invited us to join the Positive Programs school assembly group called Generation X. (The program is now called Momentum.) We had singers, dancers, and speakers as part of an hour-long assembly sharing a positive message.

I can't sing well enough to perform. I love to dance, but I can't do the kind of dancing the girls in our assemblies did. I enjoy sharing stories and encouraging others. So for this assembly program, I fit right in as one of the speakers.

You'd think I'd ease my way into the speaking thing by starting out with a few classrooms of students and then maybe I'd move up to a whole school assembly. Not me. My motto is: either go big or go home! And my first speaking engagement was a big event. I spoke to about 2,200 students at Kentwood High School.

That day, I was standing behind a black curtain with the other members of Generation X. We peeked out to watch the students file into the gym. When both sides of the bleachers were filled, I thought all of the students had arrived. But they kept coming. More and more students piled in, until the rest of the students covered the entire gym floor. Nothing like an intimidating start to my speaking profession!

MY C.L.E.A.R. MESSAGE

But it was so cool to share the stage with my brother, Zane. He sang background vocals and gave a speech encouraging the students to reach out and get to know people in their school and neighborhood. He explained about a young boy he knew with short arms and legs. At the end of his speech, he revealed that the boy was me, his little brother.

Then it was my turn to challenge each student with the mission statement of Positive Programs. I asked them this question, "Can you live to make a difference instead of dying to be accepted?" I challenge you with the same question.

After Zane went to college, I continued speaking at a few assemblies with this same group. My favorite part of the assembly was the chance to meet the students afterward so I could encourage them face-to-face. In 2007, my family established Gabriel's Foundation of HOPE, and I started speaking to schools, businesses, and churches as part of our nonprofit organization.

I came up with the C.L.E.A.R. message a few years ago. My mom and I were driving between two school assemblies. It was a busy week. We had booked seven assemblies for my four-day visit to Billings, Montana. The first assembly went really well, and right in the middle of it, I had an idea about a new message.

As we were driving, I said, "Mom, it feels like there is something missing in my program. I'm already talking about caring for fellow students with respect and excellence, but I think I should add the word 'leadership' to the mix."

We started brainstorming, and by the time we pulled up to the next school, I had my new C.L.E.A.R. message. I tried it out on that group of students, and it was a hit.

At that time, the "C" stood for Care, which is still an important part of my life mission. I really care about people, and I encourage people to have a caring heart towards others. Then one day I was reviewing my C.L.E.A.R. message, and I thought about what it takes to care about people who are different. I realized that it takes courage to get out of your comfort zone and reach out with care. I decided I wanted to show that a little courage can help you do things you've always wanted to do and make a few friends along the way. After a few assemblies, I changed the "C" in the word C.L.E.A.R. from Care to *Courage*.

The "L" became *Leadership* because I wanted to challenge the students to stand up and lead by a positive example. No matter what age group I talk to in my inspirational speeches, I believe everyone needs to understand that he or she is a leader. The challenge is to lead with a positive influence every day and keep that negative stuff out of your life.

The letter "E" has also taken on a few different meanings for me over the years. At first, it meant Excellence, because I think it is important to be excellent in whatever we set out to accomplish. But as the years have passed, I've realized that a better word for the letter "E" in my message is *Endurance*. In order to experience hope and strength in the face of life's greatest adversities, we have to have the power to last.

The "A" is for *Attitude*, and it has always been a part of my message. From the time I was a toddler, my mom and dad helped instill a positive attitude in me. I'm grateful for the way they helped me to look on the bright side of things, even when I was going through a rough time. The positive attitude I have chosen is determining the course of my future. I heard someone say that life is 80 percent attitude and 20 percent circumstance. No matter what your circumstances are, a positive attitude will get you through.

The "R" is for *Respect*. Respect has been something I've promoted for as long as I can remember. I learned as a child to respect my parents and teachers. I've always had a healthy respect for people in authority. But more importantly, I've learned that making good choices has been the best way to show respect for the life God has given me.

In the next few chapters, I'll share some stories from my life where this C.L.E.A.R. message has helped shape my hope and strength to face each day.

CHAPTER 6

C = COURAGE

Courage: the quality of mind or spirit that enables a person to face difficulty, danger, pain, etc., without fear; bravery.[1]

IT TAKES COURAGE to face life's difficulties. I have days when it takes a good deal of courage just to get up to face the day. But I know each day is a gift, and I in no way want to waste it. I will never again get to experience this hour or this day, so I choose to approach every moment with courage.

My parents were really afraid when I started junior high school. I had been in the same elementary school from kindergarten through sixth grade. We were comfortable with our routine, and I had many friends who looked out for me. But we all knew it was a whole new ball game in junior high.

In my town, three elementary schools feed into the junior high. That meant there were a couple hundred students who had never attended school with me. Some of these students had never even seen me. Would they bully me in the hall? Would I make any new friends? Would I get the same kind of help from my teachers? These were the sorts of questions that kept my mom and dad up at night worrying about this season of my life.

Sure, I wondered the same things. But I've always tried not to let that stuff scare me. I guess it's because of courage that I can go into new situations with confidence. On the first day of junior high school, I rolled my wheelchair into my first period class and felt right at home. Thankfully, Mrs. Chris Dahl was still my personal aid provided by the school district. She had been my aid since fourth grade, so she helped to make the transition process a whole lot easier.

Within the first week, I noticed a poster about a school dance coming in two weeks. I asked my mom for the five-dollar activity fee. I was excited about the chance to hang out with some of these new students after school.

When Friday came, I was ready for the challenge of attending my very first junior high school dance. The guys were standing on one side of the gym and the girls on the other. I was hanging out with my friend James and a few other guys. James asked me, "Hey, Gabe, are you going to ask anybody to dance?"

"Yeah, I was thinking about asking Danielle. You know she's the one who sits next to me in English. I'm freaking out thinking about how to ask her. Would you ask her for me?"

"I guess it's easier to ask for you than it is to ask for myself. I'll see what I can do to help you," James replied.

I watched from afar as James and Danielle talked for a while. Then James headed back to our circle of friends. My stomach was in knots. "What did she say?" I tapped my foot as I waited for his answer.

"I have some good news and some bad news," James replied. "She said she will dance with you, but she needs you to ask her. She wasn't really sweet on the idea of me asking for you."

"Boy, she doesn't want to make it easy, does she? Well, at least she said 'yes.' Now I just have to get the courage to ask her myself."

I walked through the crowd and found Danielle standing with her friends. My heart was pounding out of my chest. But I knew if I didn't ask I'd probably never have another chance. I will tell you one thing; junior high dances are not for wimps. It takes a lot of courage.

There was a noticeable difference in height between me and every other person in the gym. I stood about as tall as the other students' knees. Even though it was really scary, I tapped Danielle on the leg to get her attention and then said, "Danielle, would you like to dance with me on the next slow song?"

We stepped away from the crowd of girls, and Danielle leaned down and said, "Sure, Gabe. Just come find me when the song comes up."

I walked away with a smile and a skip in my step.

The next few songs were fast, and I paced to the beat. Then the DJ announced that the slow song was coming up next, so I found Danielle in the crowd. It was loud in the gym. She leaned down and asked, "How would you like to dance? Do you want to get your wheelchair?"

I hadn't really thought of this. She was twice as tall as I was. But it would be a little awkward for me to dance with her legs. So I bravely asked, "Danielle, would you be willing to get on your knees to dance with me?"

Guess what? She said 'yes'! Then she got down on her knees so we were the same height. My arms were too short to reach her shoulders. So she put her arms on my shoulders, and we rocked back and forth to the music.

People started circling around Danielle and me to watch us dance. I looked around and saw a group of girls staring at us. I had a moment of pride when I thought, *Hey, all you girls, I'm dancing with Danielle, so you'll have to wait your turn.*

Because of courage, I had a great time at the dance and many other junior high school activities. I'm glad I had the courage to take the risk and ask a girl to dance. It turned out to be a really great time. Danielle and I remained friends all throughout our junior high years.

A few weeks after the dance, I auditioned for the school play.

C = COURAGE

I got a speaking part as an animal in *The Lion, the Witch and the Wardrobe*, the play based on the book by C. S. Lewis. I chose to be a squirrel. With my short arms and bent knees, I actually sort of resemble a squirrel. My mom made me a furry costume and painted my face gray. Looking back at the photos, I can't believe I did it, but it was a fun time.

As part of the drama team, I had another opportunity to meet people and make new friends. I also learned about courage from this play. The main characters of the story are Peter, Susan, Edmund, and Lucy. They receive their courage from Aslan the Lion. In the same way, when I need courage, I talk to God and ask for the courage and grace to do what I need to do, and He provides it.

While we were rehearsing for the play, I noticed a flyer about basketball tryouts. I loved watching Zane play basketball. He taught me how to dribble and showed me some of the plays he learned when he played basketball for Leota Junior High.

I later asked my mom if I could try out for the seventh grade team. She looked at me as if I had asked her to fly me to the moon.

"Mom, come on! You know I can dribble the ball like crazy. You see me when I play with Zane. I know I can do it." I used my best persuasive speech techniques to convince her it was a great idea.

Mom and Dad finally agreed to let me try out after we talked to the coach to make sure he thought it was okay. He was cool with it. The rest of the team agreed it was okay to change things up a little to accommodate my needs.

The day Coach Benjamin said he'd let me play was one of the best days of my life. I made the team. I was so excited to be a Leota Lion basketball player.

Because of the rehearsals for the school play, I had to miss a few of the basketball practices. Coach Benjamin said I had to follow the district rule of participating in ten practices, just like the other kids, before he would let me play. No favoritism for me. I liked that. For some reason it just makes me feel more "normal" when people don't bend the rules for me. The other guys on the team thought it was cool that I wanted to play.

We tried on my uniform, and it was a little big. No, it was huge. But I didn't care. I was officially a Leota Lion basketball player. We pinned up the sleeves and decided I would wear a pair of my shorts. I didn't want to risk the school uniform shorts falling off while I was hopping down the court. That would not have been cool.

I finally get to wear a real school basketball uniform. I can't believe I am on a school team just like Zane. These were the thoughts rolling around inside my head all night long before my first game.

Mom agreed to drive me to the game. I didn't want to pull up to my first basketball game in a short bus. You know about the short bus, don't you? In our district, it is equipped with wheelchair access and is used for all special needs students. We call it the "B" bus. It seemed silly to have a whole bus just for me. Mom's van was much more normal.

We arrived early, and I parked my wheelchair in the corner of the gym. I then scooted into the locker room to get ready for my first career basketball game. I was probably more nervous than the day I asked Danielle to dance. It takes courage to play sports. But I knew I had to push through my fear because I really love basketball.

While we were warming up, I noticed the kids from the other team staring at me and not paying attention to their drills. One guy rammed into one of his fellow players because he was focusing on me and not on the drill. I suppose they had no idea how I was going to play basketball standing three feet tall with three-inch arms. Soon I'd show them just how capable I was on the court when I started dribbling and passing the ball.

Our team wasn't very good, but we had a lot of fun. I didn't score any baskets. But it was a sweet moment when I dribbled the ball in from the end of the court and passed it off to Brendon James, who swished the ball in the basket for a three-point shot. My name made it into the playbook that day, with an assist marked next to it. That moment was one of the highlights of my seventh-grade year. I didn't think it could get any better than that.

The day of our last game, Michael King of *King 5 News* of Seattle showed up at Canyon Park Junior High. His camera guy filmed the game, and they interviewed me and a few of the other players. I felt like a celebrity! We almost won that game, but we lost in the last seconds. It didn't bother me that we lost. I still thought it was a blast.

The station produced a story for the evening news titled "Gabe, the Lionhearted." The story featured some great video of our game and an interview of my friend Brendon, my mom, and me. It was pretty cool.

A few months after my basketball story hit the news, the *Seattle Times* newspaper did a feature article about my life, written by Cara Solomon.[2] This article hit the street on my thirteenth birthday. I had a group of guys spend the night for my birthday, and it was so fun to wake up and see my story on the cover of the paper.

The whole day was incredible because I also got to throw out the first pitch at the Seattle Mariners game. When we arrived at Safeco field to check in at the front desk, the receptionist practically jumped out of her chair and said, "Oh, thank God you are here! *Good Morning America* has been calling all day, trying to get in touch with you." She handed mom a piece of paper with the number for the *ABC Television Studio*.

Mom dialed the number and left a message on voice-mail. Then we were escorted out onto Safeco field. There was energy in the air. We had about sixty friends and family at the game to witness the event. Mom, dad, Zane, my cousin Katy, my uncle Russ, and some of my basketball team friends joined me on the third baseline.

About a minute before I hopped out to the pitcher's mound, a girl ran up to Mom and handed her a cell phone. "It's *Good Morning America* again. They want to talk to you."

Right about then, the announcer started to introduce me. On the giant screen they played some of the *King 5 News* basketball story. Then he said, "Ladies and gentlemen, please join me in welcoming Gabe Murfitt."

After I heard my name, adrenaline pumped through me. I jumped over the third-base line and hopped out onto the soft grass. I looked around and thought, *Wow, there are a lot of people.* They were on their feet, clapping and screaming. I looked at Randy Winn, who was at home plate and ready to catch my pitch.

I pitched the ball as hard as I could. It one-hopped to the plate, and everybody erupted in applause when Randy caught it. He ran out to me and handed me the ball. Then we posed for a picture.

I walked back across the infield and jumped over the third-base line into my dad's arms. It was one of the most unforgettable moments of my life.

When we got up to our seats, Mom told me about the phone call from *Good Morning America*. They asked if I'd be willing to give them first rights to my story. They planned to fly us to New York as soon as possible.

"Are you kidding me, Mom? *Good Morning America*? How did they find out about me? You said 'yes,' didn't you?"

As it turned out, they found out about me because of the *Seattle Times* article.

We didn't end up flying to New York. They postponed us for a couple of weeks because that night some hostages were released, and they took my spot on the show. That was okay by me. By then, I was a little overwhelmed by all this attention—the *King 5* news story, the

C = COURAGE

Seattle Times article, and throwing the first pitch were highlights of my year. I had no idea it would get even more fun.

A few weeks later, we had a *Good Morning America* camera crew and the show's producer, Brian O'Keefe, at our house. These guys were very nice and spent three days following me around school. It was a little bizarre having a big camera in my face that was recording everything I said. But it was also fun to think I'd be on television sharing my story to help other kids live with courage.

Good Morning America aired my story in June 2003. Brian put together a nice video that covered my family and friends, my school, my baseball team, and the infamous dance with Danielle. I watched it at school during home room, and we all thought it was good.

Zane and I were also on a local sports talk show titled *Tony Ventrella Tonight*. Then the Northwest Cable News network did a follow-up story that covered a day when thirteen people helped me climb to Camp Muir at the base camp of Mt. Rainier. That's a story of endurance I'll tell in a later chapter.

During this season of my life, my mom was doing a Bible study. She told me about a very courageous guy named Joshua. I love how God reminded Joshua to be strong and courageous. When I find myself losing courage, I read this Bible verse:

> Have I not commanded you? Be strong and courageous. Do not be afraid; do not be discouraged, for the LORD your God will be with you wherever you go.
>
> —Joshua 1:9

I believe that God will be with me wherever I go. This truth gives me great courage. I know that with God by my side, I can accomplish the dreams in my heart.

I tell you these stories to encourage you to get out of your comfort zone. Gather up some courage, and try whatever you've always ⅃med of doing. Have you always wanted to play a sport? Do you want to try out for a school play or audition for *American Idol*? Is there something you need to talk to your parents about? Do you want to apply for a job? Go for it! God will give you all the courage you need. Just ask.

I love to dribble the basketball and play point guard.
(Photo by Jim Bates)

C = COURAGE

It takes courage to be a squirrel in *The Lion, the Witch and the Wardrobe*.

Courage Challenge

- Be brave enough to follow your dreams.
- Be courageous and reach out to someone who needs a friend.
- Be persistent as you figure out a way to learn a new thing.
- Be bold and speak the truth.
- Be willing to ask for help.

CHAPTER 7

L = LEADERSHIP

Leadership: the position or function of a leader, a person who guides or directs a group: ability to lead[3]

Leadership is ultimately about creating a way for people to contribute to making something extraordinary happen.[4]

—*Alan Keith of Genentech*

THERE ARE MANY leaders who lead by example and show me how to live a positive and effective life. I'm a better person because these leaders came into my life. I call them "my heroes."

When I was in elementary school, I looked up to the older kids. Well, yes, I literally looked up to them because I'm so short, but what I mean is that I admired them. I wanted to be like them. They were bigger and stronger, and most of them were smarter. I stayed away from a few of them who didn't set a very good example, but for the most part, these older kids in my school were cool.

Where I live, the junior high school is seventh through ninth grade. So I looked up to the ninth graders because they were the top dogs of the school. I especially liked the students who took time to check in and say "hi." They led with great care and compassion and weren't afraid to reach out to include me in conversations and show me they cared.

L = LEADERSHIP

In high school, the seniors were headed toward college or a job, and they were on my radar screen. I learned a great deal about what to do and what not to do simply by observing these students. My favorite leaders were the people who waited to open a door for me or took time to sit with me at lunch. It wasn't always the star athlete or the most popular girl who made my top leader list; it was those who took time to care.

My challenge to you is to be a caring leader right where you are. It doesn't matter how old you are. There are so many people who need a positive influence in their lives. They might just be waiting for someone like you.

I also encourage you to be a friend to someone in need. Your friendship can make a difference in a life headed toward disaster. Suicide has touched my family in more ways than I ever dreamed. It is one of the major killers of young people these days, but it doesn't have to be. If each one of us took the time to be a positive leader and reach out to others, we could make a significant difference in the lives of those around us. Your caring influence might save a life.

Zane has been a leader to me all my life. He encourages me to try new things. He influences me as I watch him make good choices. He takes care of his body. He worked hard to finish college strong, and now he has a good job where he honors his employer. It is important to him to make God a priority in his life. He wasn't always following the crowd; he was leading the way.

I was proud when Zane was voted the most inspirational player on the high school varsity football team. He may not have been the star quarterback, but he was the star encourager. He challenged the other Woodinville Falcons to work hard and give their all for every game.

When I watched how Zane dealt with being cut from the basketball team, I learned about how to handle disappointment.

He chose not to whine and complain. Instead, he rallied behind the team and became the loudest guy in the stands as he was cheering on his fellow teammates.

When he didn't make the all-star baseball team, he didn't hold a grudge or talk nasty about the coaches who made the decision not to pick him. Instead, he volunteered to help them practice, knowing he'd never be a part of the team. Now that's what I call leading with a positive example!

I want to be like Zane. I know he is going to continue to be a leader of influence. It is an honor to have a brother like him who will lead me throughout my life.

Take a minute to think about this question: is there someone in your life who wants to be just like you? Are you living in such a way that people admire your actions? I sure hope so, because whether you know it or not, you are a leader. Do you know who is watching? Are you leading them to places you want them to follow? Are you a good influence? If not, now is the time to make a change. It is never too late to turn the other way if the path you are on is not getting you to a positive place.

I have made the decision to live in such a way that I make a difference in the world. I don't want to die following someone else's poor choices, just to be accepted by my friends. I don't need to be a bully or a partier or do drugs just to be cool. It can be tempting because it seems that's what the popular kids do. But I want to be a leader who chooses to say "no" to these destructive things. I'd rather make good choices and live with no regrets.

I've watched too many people in my life as they struggled to figure out who they are. They do things they never dreamed they would do, just to be liked by their friends or to hide from their pain. Then it turns out that it wasn't worth it because the consequences are very painful. It makes me really sad to watch people go through this cycle. Don't do it!

L = LEADERSHIP

When I was in college, I went through a time where I didn't make good choices. I wasn't honest with my parents, and I was participating in activities that were inappropriate and unhealthy. I also took shortcuts in school where I could. It was not a fun time.

I'm thankful I didn't stay in that dark place very long. I faced the truth of what I was doing and talked to my parents about it. Then I surrounded myself with people who could help me stay accountable to my goals. I joined a group of young men at my church, and we still help each other through the struggles of life.

I want to encourage you that no matter where you are or what decisions you've made, there is always a path back to the best plan for your life. Life is too short to stay on a detour for long. Get back on track, and move forward toward your dreams.

Every life is significant, especially yours. We were made by God to do great things, not to compromise and live a life designed by the world's selfish standards. I challenge you to realize that God's ways are so much higher than any ways we design ourselves. I hope you choose to live an extraordinary life and become a positive influence on those around you. A good leader helps bring the best out of the people he or she influences.

I've learned to be a successful leader by following the great examples of some other leaders I have come to know. These people chose the better way and encouraged others along their paths. Their choices made them excellent leaders and world-changers.

Be a Friendly Leader

I have heard people say that their high school years were the best years of their life. Boy, not for me. I'd rather get a root canal than go back to high school. Don't get me wrong, I had some good times, but I had a lot of days when I sat through my lunch hour alone. Most of my weekends were spent at home with my family, when I would have preferred being out having fun with friends.

The kids I hung out with in junior high made new friends by the time they got to high school. It felt like they were not sure how to act around me anymore. They weren't mean to me. They just ignored me—no eye contact or "Hey, Gabe" as they passed me in the hall at school. They no longer asked how my day was going. It was heartbreaking, and I dreaded going to school.

Some days I felt invisible. I didn't understand why some kids who talked to me in junior high didn't acknowledge me on the way to classes in high school. I can't even remember how many times I waited outside in a hallway for someone to help me open the door if Mrs. Dahl wasn't there to open it for me. It surprised me when kids walked past, opened the door, and let it close before I had a chance to get my wheelchair through. It was the indifference of people that made it difficult.

During this time, I complained to my mom and dad. I had a hard time understanding why I was not being invited to the parties I was hearing about at school. Didn't people care enough to invite me to a movie? Why couldn't we just hang out and play Xbox? People noticed my broken body, but no one saw my broken heart. I was not happy.

It is highly likely that you've experienced similar feelings in your life. I'm sorry if that is true for you. Please tell someone how you are feeling. Don't isolate yourself in your struggles. Just like I do, you have some choices to make when you face difficulties.

I chose to control my attitude and my responses to the people around me. I chose to be a positive influence even when I was hurting. I could make that choice because I knew God would make a way to help me through my difficult times. He had done it before, and I knew He would do it again.

As I struggled with my loneliness, my mom made me an appointment with our counselor, Karen Bartsch. She helped me to realize that it wasn't the end of the world. There was a lot of partying going on at my school, and she asked me to consider if I really wanted to be involved with that kind of behavior. She constantly reminded me to trust God and that He would work things for my good. She said that He would eventually give me good friends, but maybe I was looking for them in the wrong places. Maybe I wasn't reaching out to people who could have a positive influence on my life. Perhaps God was calling me to initiate friendships with other kids. She challenged me to get back into a small group at my church, where I'd have some accountability partners. I've learned she was right.

I couldn't see this then, but now as I look back, I believe that God was protecting me during my high school years. Because I can't drive, I have to rely on someone to get me to and from events. This puts me in jeopardy if my friends decide to drink and drive. What if something had happened at a party and I needed to get away but no one would help me? After mulling it over and choosing to think this way, I'm settled with the idea that, once again, God had my back and was protecting me.

One of the other things I learned during these lonely times was how important it is to talk it out with someone who can help. Talk to a friend, your parents, a guidance counselor, a teacher, or a pastor if you are struggling. Sometimes it takes a different perspective to help you see what is really going on.

Mr. Segadelli

Some of my teachers helped me in that way. Mr. Segadelli, my high school health teacher, convinced me that drinking alcohol wasn't a good idea. He showed us a chart comparing how much we weighed to the number of beers it would take to get above the legal limit of blood-alcohol rate. Since I weigh about seventy-five pounds, I'd be in trouble after barely one drink. When he showed me this truth, I made a conscious choice: I decided I was not interested in going to the parties where people got drunk. It wasn't worth the risk. I didn't need that junk in my life. I'd already seen how it destroyed friends and family members.

I am glad for mentors like Mr. Segadelli. Teachers who speak the truth and don't try to be best friends with their students teach the greatest lessons. I was grateful to have many teachers with this leadership skill.

Please understand that not everything about high school was bad. I had a few good friends who were part of the marching band. My friend Jeremy Supinski was a year older than I was. He was willing to hang out with me, so that helped. Sarah and Victoria Severin were good friends too. They also went to my church. I went to the homecoming dance with Victoria and the prom with Sarah. I had a great time because they were willing to reach out and be my friend. I'm thankful for caring and courageous people who took time to get to know me.

I want to make note that I wasn't the only student who struggled in school. I observed kids who were bullied because of the color of their hair, choice of clothing, their height or weight, their ethnic background, or because they had piercings or tattoos. Regardless of the form of mistreatment, it made and still makes me sad. I challenge you to make a difference by being a leader who treats everyone with respect. Be a leader who has no tolerance for bullying.

Rather than sitting back and being a victim of what other kids do or don't do, take the lead and make a difference in the outcome of your life. Invite friends over to watch a sporting event or play video games. Organize a night at the movies, or pull some friends together to go bowling. It may sound risky, but I know it will be worth it. You might change a life. Set a goal to make a new friend. Then you'll settle the loneliness issue for two people.

L = LEADERSHIP

Cal Ripken, Jr.

When I think about amazing leaders, one person who comes to my mind is Cal Ripken, Jr. He is a famous baseball player who played in the major leagues for the Baltimore Orioles from 1981 to 2001. He played in 2,632 games without ever missing a game. Now that takes hard work and leadership and endurance!

In February of my eighth-grade year, I was sitting in the cafeteria at school. One of the ninth-grade girls sat at the table with me and a couple of my friends. She said she was taking a survey for our school video production class, the Lion Channel. She asked us to give her a list of our heroes. I listed several athletes, including Emmitt Smith, Carlos Delgado, and Cal Ripken, Jr.

I learned later that my mom had asked our vice-principal, Mr. Farquhar, to help get a list of my heroes. I had no idea that the information was going to be given to the producer of *The Oprah Winfrey Show.*

The producer had contacted my mom after reading about me on the Internet. A whole camera crew spent a day at my house filming my story in October 2003, but they decided not to have me on the show for a few months. Instead, the producers chose me for a show about real-life superheroes. That was why mom needed that list of my heroes.

In May 2004, we flew to Chicago for the taping of the show. We arrived a day early because the producers wanted to update some of the video to fit the real-life superhero segment. In the Harpo production studio (Harpo is Oprah spelled backwards), we recorded a short segment where I talked about several of my heroes. It was fun to be in the studio and walk on the set where Oprah filmed the show each day.

We could barely sleep that night. I never dreamed I'd be sitting on the couch next to Oprah Winfrey. The morning of the show, butterflies were making my stomach flip out while my mom helped me get dressed.

The van picked us up about four hours before show time. That gave them time to set up microphones and get us ready to answer Oprah's questions. It also gave the makeup artists time to work their magic. My mom's thick, curly hair was a big ball of frizz in the humid Chicago air. They straight ironed it, and I hardly recognized her. Then they put makeup on all of us. Yes, that's right. Even my dad, my brother, and I got our faces powdered. I thought that part was gross.

As we prepared for the show, we learned we would be on the set with Kirsten Dunst and Tobey Maguire, the main cast of the movie *Spider-Man 2*. Sony Pictures was sponsoring the show to promote the movie.

Oprah's five real-life superheroes and our families waited in the green room until it was time to set up in the audience. The celebrities had a separate green room. Jen, our producer, brought us onto the set, where the audience was practicing their cheers with a set producer. Jen escorted us to our seats—right in front of Oprah's couch. By now my stomach was really dancing the butterfly dance.

Loud cheers erupted when Oprah walked onto the set. The place went nuts with clapping and cheering. It was louder than Safeco field after Griffey hit a homerun. The audience was filled mostly with out-of-control women who cried at the sight of Oprah. That was a little weird to me, but I sat back and enjoyed the fun.

First we watched a clip from the *Spider-Man 2* movie. Then Oprah introduced Tobey and Kirsten. I can't even remember what they talked about because I was so nervous getting ready for my part. Everything moved so fast.

Soon, Oprah introduced her real-life superheroes one by one. I was number three. During a commercial break, Zane carried me down the stairs and set me on Oprah's couch. I wondered if the audience could hear my thumping heart in the microphone that was attached to my shirt.

Oprah told the audience about me and played the video the producer had filmed at our house. Then Oprah said, "Please welcome Gabe Murfitt."

I was a little embarrassed when the whole audience stood up clapping. It was really loud in my hearing aid. My mom and dad were sitting right in front of me, grinning from ear to ear. Mom was trying to wipe her tears away without messing up her makeup.

After all the noise died down, Oprah asked me a few questions. She began, "Was there never a time when you felt like you were very different and that you were depressed about it? Was there never a time?"

I responded, "When I was younger, I finally figured out I was different and I wasn't going to change. But I'm happy with the way that I am."

"What do you do when people stare?"

"I just give them a smile. When they come up to me and ask me what's wrong, I tell them why my arms are short and why my knees are bent. I can't straighten them. So I just let people know what's up."

"Well, this is the thing. When we told a friend of ours your story, he hopped on a plane to come and meet you in person. Ladies and gentlemen, the legendary Cal Ripken."

During this time, my hearing aid was buzzing from the sound of the studio lights. I didn't hear some of what Oprah was saying. She was saying something about my hero, Cal Ripken, Jr., but I didn't understand why the audience started clapping until I saw him walk out onto the set.

He was bigger than life. At six-feet, four inches tall, he towered over Oprah when he gave her a hug. Then he walked right up and knelt down in front of me. Even on his knees he was way bigger than I was.

MY MESSAGE IS C.L.E.A.R.

His eyes were crystal blue, and he was smiling. He was carrying a black baseball bat with his name signed in silver right on the sweet spot of the bat. I was speechless. My mind was racing so much I didn't pay attention to what he said at first. It was crazy!

Once the audience quieted down, he looked me right in the eye and said, "Gabe, when I heard about you, I was so inspired by your courage and your spirit that I had to jump on a plane and come and meet you in person and let you know that you're my hero."

I couldn't believe it!

Then he said, "I also brought you this. Since I'm retired now and I'm not using this anymore, I decided to bring you one of my bats to present to you."

The only word that could come out of my mouth was, "Thanks."

Oprah said, "Oh that's good. We asked Cal if he wanted to send a tape, but he said, 'No, I want to come meet him in person.'"

The audience started freaking out again.

Then Oprah asked, "So what does it feel like to be sitting next to your hero who says you're his hero?"

I replied, "I don't know. It's indescribable. I'm sitting next to one of the best baseball players to ever play the game."

Oprah smiled. "Yeah! And I think Cal has another surprise for Gabe and his brother, Zane."

As Cal started to talk, Oprah went into the audience and grabbed my brother's hand and escorted him to the couch.

Zane sat between me and Kirsten Dunst. Cal was on my left. Oprah stood near my parents. I really felt like I was in some sort of a dream.

When the commercial ended, they played a video of Cal's state-of-the-art baseball fields in Aberdeen, Maryland. It showed him coaching some young kids on how to hold the bat. The fields looked like professional ball fields.

L = LEADERSHIP

I wasn't sure why we were watching this video, but then Cal explained, "I love the relationship you have with your brother. I too have a similar relationship. I'd like to extend an invitation to you to come to my complex in Maryland. It is a brand-new, fabulous complex. Bring your brother, Zane, and my brother Billy and I will help you become better baseball players."

Both Zane and I were shocked. There was lots of clapping, and then it was over.

Oprah thanked everybody, and we moved on to the next hero. Cal joined us in the audience and sat next to me and Zane. We chatted during commercials. It was awesome.

I kept wondering what else was going to happen. Oprah was full of surprises, and once again, she didn't let me down.

To close out the show, she asked Kirsten and Tobey to share another surprise. We learned that Sony Pictures was flying us to Los Angeles to attend the premier of *Spider-Man 2* and walk the red carpet with all the Hollywood movie stars. We were invited to the after-party at the Santa Monica Pier too. They also told us we would receive a Spider-Man goody box when we got home. (A few weeks later, a box twice my size arrived. It was filled with every Spider-Man toy you could think of. It was crazy!)

"Oh my gosh! Unbelievable." That's all I could say.

When the show was over, we spent time taking photos and saying "good-bye" to all the amazing heroes we met that day.

A month later, on June 22, 2004, we flew to Los Angeles for the *Spider-Man 2* movie premiere and party. It was over the top with total Hollywood style. I about went blind when the paparazzi snapped photos of Zane and me walking on the red carpet. Our limo took us to the Santa Monica pier after the movie. There was a giant Spider-Man on the Ferris wheel, and the arcade games and prizes were transformed into a Spidey theme.

MY MESSAGE IS C.L.E.A.R.

We mingled with the stars until two o'clock in the morning. My mom and dad celebrated their wedding anniversary that day too. I was glad to give them a special trip. Well, it actually was paid for by Sony Pictures and Oprah, so I can't claim that I gave it to them. But they thanked me anyway.

A month later, we headed to Aberdeen, Maryland, and had the time of our lives with about two hundred and fifty other baseball campers. It was totally a dream come true and more than I could have ever imagined. I got to practice with Cal and Billy Ripken and other professional coaches. I also met a group of nice young guys with funny East Coast accents.

Comcast SportsNet showed up and did a story about how Cal and Billy brought me and Zane to their camp. It was a great segment that played on the evening news. Later that year, it won an Emmy Award. There was also a Japanese reporter and camera crew there. I never got to see that story, but I'd love to hear a voice-over of me talking in Japanese.

So what makes Cal Ripken, Jr. such a great leader? He worked hard at the game of baseball and was no slacker. He set an example for his fellow teammates as a model player, and his devotion to his job was undeniably great. And even since he retired, he has spent time helping young baseball players succeed through his training programs and camps. He's always helping others achieve greatness. That is why he is one of my heroes.

Mr. Ed Hogle

My elementary school PE teacher was also a great leader of influence in my life. I loved having Mr. Hogle as a teacher. He was willing to help me figure out ways to participate in class when other teachers worried that I wasn't capable. He challenged me to get out on the basketball court and practice dribbling. He let me play goalie in floor hockey. Together we stretched our imaginations to accommodate for my disability. Boy, that was fun! He helped me see my true potential.

I loved it when we did the shuttle run. The object of the game was to run the course in the fastest time. I'd run (hop on my butt) a few feet and pick up an eraser and bring it back to the starting line. Then I had to run a few feet further and pick up another eraser to bring back to the beginning point. You get the drill?

It was so much fun for me to hop down to the first line, pick up the eraser, and hop down to the next line. Mr. Hogle yelled out my times to motivate me to go faster. Adrenaline pumped through my veins. My lungs were gasping for air. Every time we played the shuttle run, I'd try to beat my previous time. One time I was behind a few seconds from my previous record, so I threw the eraser at the finish line, trying to beat the clock.

Mr. Hogle gave me "the look," and I was busted. He was a good sport and reminded me that my body needed to cross the line, not just the eraser.

What I appreciated most about him was that he gave me a chance. He didn't make me go to the library during PE or ask me to sit out a round of basketball. Instead, we figured out how I could participate in my own way.

Being creative and stretching your imagination is another great tool of a leader. I hope that someday I'll be able to help young people push their limits by encouraging them to try new things. Mr. Hogle set a good example for me to follow.

Now that I've shared about a couple of great leaders in my life, I hope you will think about the qualities of a leader and aspire to be one too.

What kind of leader do you want to be? I imagine you will be a great leader who will change the world. Be courageous, and take the steps to lead with a positive example. Someone is waiting for you to lead the way.

My favorite leader who leads with a positive attitude is Joni Eareckson Tada. This photo was taken at the Joni and Friends Family Camp in the summer of 2011.
Front row (L–R): Ruth, Gabe, and Joni Eareckson Tada
Back row (L–R): Chris Seideman (a really cool guy who volunteered to be my short-term missionary at the camp), Mom, Ken Tada, and Dad.

L = LEADERSHIP

Leadership Challenge

- Live to make a difference; don't die to be accepted.
- Lead by a positive example, and make good choices.
- Learn from other great leaders.
- Look for ways to encourage lonely people.
- Live with no regrets.

CHAPTER 8

E = ENDURANCE

Endurance: the fact or power of enduring or bearing pain, or hardships. It is the ability or strength to continue to last, especially despite fatigue, stress or other adverse conditions.[5]

If you think you can do a thing or think you can't do a thing, you're right.[6]
—*Henry Ford*

WHAT COMES TO your mind when you think of the word "endurance"? I once heard someone say that endurance means passionate patience. In my mind, I see a picture of my cousin Katy Goodheart Sears at about the twenty-mile mark of the Portland Marathon. She's been pushing the limit, and she has 6.2 miles to go. She needs incredible strength and endurance to run that far. She has endured painful blisters on her feet, the loss of her toenails, and muscle aches beyond what I can even imagine. Yet she keeps going strong.

I watched her run the marathon in Portland, Oregon, which was one of the first of several marathons she would finish. This past year, Katy also ran the Boston Marathon. She trained and finished the race with a smile on her face, almost as if she was ready for more!

My friend Laura Clavero also ran in the Boston Marathon. Her stepdaughter, Natalie, plays on my baseball team. It made me happy because Laura wore a T-shirt with the logo for Gabriel's Foundation of HOPE on the back. She was running to bring awareness of our family's nonprofit organization.

My muscles hurt just thinking about running that far. The furthest I've gone on my scooter is seven miles, and I hurt for a couple days afterwards. I really can't imagine running 26.2 miles. My hat is off to all you marathon runners. Your ability to endure inspires me.

Another thought comes to mind when I think of endurance. It is a memory of a hot June day in 2003 when twelve people hiked for six hours to get to Camp Muir on Mount Rainier. (Check out this link to learn more about Camp Muir: http://www.nps.gov/mora/parknews/camp-muir-webcam.htm.) These friends and family members trained for this hike so I could have an opportunity to see Washington and Oregon from a 10,188-foot elevation.

As we climbed, each of the men took turns carrying me in a backpack. We let my mom and my aunt Kathy off the hook for carrying me, but they climbed the mountain with everyone else. Once we hit the snow glacier, the guys took turns pulling me in a sled that attached to their waists. They worked hard, dragging me up the glacier while I took a nap. Now that was easy!

Once we got to Camp Muir, everyone was pretty worn out, but the view was worth it. We could see for miles. I remember sitting in the camp area eating my lunch and feeling grateful for the sacrifice they made just for me. They endured aching muscles and sore feet so I could climb such a beautiful mountain. I looked at my dad and said, "I'll remember this for the rest of my life."

I imagine you can think of several people in your life who have endured. I have many family members who have helped me see that endurance is an important key to a successful life. I think it is amazing that I'm part of a community of people who can help me in every area of my life. I hope you can tap into a community like mine.

Two of my aunts, Shelley Devine Davison and Patti Devine Beckwith, and my great-aunt Nina Murfitt Krakenberg endured the long process of being healed from cancer. They chose to endure each day of their treatment with hope. I am thankful that they are healed.

Our good friends, Randy and Rod Halvorson have spent most of their lives in wheelchairs because of muscular dystrophy. They are twins living with a degenerative disease that slowly takes away muscle control year by year. They turned fifty-three years old in 2011 and are therefore two of the oldest living people with this disease. Yet they endure. I love spending time with them because they inspire me to make the best of each day. Although they have limited use of their bodies, they live lives full of activity, including coaching basketball and softball. I've learned from their positive attitudes and ability to endure.

Joni Eareckson Tada (http://www.joniandfriends.org) dove into a lake when she was seventeen years old and broke her neck. The injury resulted in quadriplegia. She has endured over four decades with limited use of most of her body. Yet she lives a life more inspired than most able-bodied people. She started the Joni and Friends International Disability Center and serves people with disabilities all over the world.

Someday I'd like to travel with one of Joni's teams to deliver wheelchairs to people like me who live in other countries where wheelchairs are difficult to obtain. Take the time to check out her website and learn more about her incredible worldwide ministry. Maybe you can join me on one of the mission trips.

I have learned a great deal about endurance from my grandma Helen Devine (my mom's mother). She was severely injured in an accident when she was sixteen years old. An eighteen-inch thick fire curtain fell from the ceiling of the junior high auditorium and crushed her spine. Although she was eventually able to walk, she always struggled with pain and a severe limp.

Not only did Grandma Helen endure her disability, but also she endured the heartache of the early deaths of several family members. One of these people was my grandpa Bob Devine. He died from lung cancer when he was only forty-eight years old. Grandma Helen was left to raise ten children on her own. She endured this hardship with grace and a smile. I really learned a lot from her.

Recently I met man who endured 2,103 days as a prisoner of war in a communist prison. Captain Charlie Plumb was a fighter pilot serving our country when he was shot down in Vietnam. He lived through unbelievable torture and hardship. His military honors include two Purple Hearts, the Legion of Merit, the Silver Star, the Bronze Star, and the POW Medal. His faith and hope inspire me to consider each day a gift and to give it everything I've got. I encourage you to read Charlie's book titled *I'm No Hero*. He may not think so, but I think he is truly a hero and a perfect example of endurance. I'd like to give him a C.L.E.A.R. medal for endurance. Check out his webpage at http://www.CharliePlumb.com.

I could fill the rest of the pages of this book with the stories of people who have endured through a long list of challenges. I think we can learn by reading other people's stories. I hope the stories I have told provided you with a little extra motivation to endure. They inspire me to keep going when the going is tough.

When I think of endurance in my life, I have several areas where passionate patience has helped me. Sometimes the simple act of getting dressed is difficult. I've learned to persevere when I can't pull my shirt over my head or pull my pants over my knee. I keep trying until I get it right. I don't give up easily. I endure until I figure out a way.

When I first started to dress myself, it took more than half an hour to get dressed. With perseverance, I've figured out creative ways to use my dressing stick to speed up the process. It is a long, wooden stick with a hook on the end that helps me pull up my pants. I've learned to wiggle just right to pull my shirt over my head. Now I can get dressed in less than ten minutes. Speedy!

Hard times are just a part of life. I don't know anyone who hasn't gone through difficult days. But not everyone stays strong and endures through to the end. Some people give up too soon. Endurance requires believing with hope that each day is a gift worth opening. I make a choice to endure every day. In fact, my whole life has been a lesson in endurance. The last several years have taught me the most in this area.

After my lonely high school years, I was looking forward to a change. I applied to go to college at both the University of Washington and the University of Montana. I always had a dream of going to the University of Washington. It is near where I live, and I have been a Husky fan since I was in elementary school.

In my sophomore year of high school, I was accepted to a great program for people with disabilities at the University of Washington called Do-It (http://www.washington.edu/doit). Through this program, I was able to experience campus life by staying in the dorms at the University for a couple of weeks. I was a part of Do-It during the summers of high school. This really increased my Husky fever.

My heart was set on becoming a University of Washington Husky. I didn't have super good grades, so I doubted I would make it into such a great school. After I submitted my application, I said a lot of prayers, hoping to be accepted.

Toward the end of my senior year of high school, my classmates were getting their college letters of acceptance. I had been accepted to the University of Montana, where both of my parents got their degrees, but I was still checking the mailbox every day in search of that acceptance letter to the University of Washington.

One day after school, my mom dropped me off at home and headed back to work. It was a daily ritual for me to check the University of Washington website to see if there was any news about my application. When I saw the word "ACCEPTED" on the application page, I jumped off the computer chair and did a happy dance. I screamed so loud that I scared Donovan, the family dog. I thought we both were going to have a heart attack.

E = ENDURANCE

I picked up the phone and dialed my mom's number. "Mom, are you sitting down?"

"What's going on, Gabe?" Mom replied. "Is everything okay?"

"You're not going to believe this. Right after you dropped me off, I checked the U-Dub website. I got in! Mom, I'm going to be a Husky! The website says my status is accepted."

"Wow, Gabe, I'm proud of you. Congratulations!"

"I'm going to see if my packet came in the mail. I'll see you when you get home."

I called Dad, and he was even more excited than Mom. Then I opened the door into the garage to head out to the mailbox. My heart sank. No wheelchair. I left it in the van that my mom took back to her office.

I didn't want to wait for Mom to get home, so I walked (scooting on my butt) up the long driveway to get to the mailbox. It took me a while, but I made it. Without my wheelchair, I wasn't tall enough to reach the mailbox, so I found a brick in the neighbor's garden and stood on it to make me just the right height to reach the mail.

I unfolded a large envelope. *Yes! It is addressed to Gabriel Steven Murfitt.* That's me! The Husky logo in the corner made my heart do a flip-flop. I practically ran back down the driveway. I didn't care if I scraped the skin off my ankle.

Once I was back inside, I took a deep breath and opened the envelope. Then I read the most amazing statement of my life: "Congratulations! You have been accepted to the University of Washington for the fall quarter of 2008!"

Once again, I did my happy dance. *Holy cow! Oh my gosh! Yes, God! I did it! I'm a Husky! Go Dawgs! Bow down to Washington! Go Huskies! Go Huskies!*

I read the letter over and over again. They accepted me on the condition that I enroll in a special program for "at risk" students called the STP (Summer Transition Program). I was required to spend four weeks on the University of Washington campus, taking summer classes to make sure I could handle a school with such high academic standards.

I really didn't care if they made me stand on my head all day. I'd do whatever it took to be a Husky! My dream was coming true.

The summer program was a success, thanks to a group of people from the University's Office of Minority Affairs and Diversity. They kept us all on track while encouraging us not to give up. I made new friends with students who were committed to helping each other make it at the University of Washington. I really did well over the four weeks of living on campus, even though it was really hard for my mom and dad to let me go. It was the first time I had been away from them for that long.

After such a great summer, I knew it was going to be a good year. I could feel it in my bones. All the struggles I had been through in high school faded away with the hope for a good future. I was excited to live in the dorms and make some new friends.

One of my other dreams was to play in the University of Washington marching band. I started playing drums in the fifth grade. I was in orchestra and concert band, but my favorite was marching band. I love the pomp and circumstance. I envisioned being part of the elite Husky drumline, wearing that purple and gold uniform.

Early in the summer, I registered for an audition to join the squad. I practiced the difficult, required musical pieces and learned the new cadences. Because my thumbs don't work, I have to drum with my sticks between my pointer and middle fingers. My hands gets tired, but I usually can keep up with the rhythm.

As the day for auditions approached, I was both nervous and excited. There were about fifteen drummers trying out for ten available positions on the drumline. Even the drummers who made the squad in prior years had to try out again. I thought I might have a decent shot if I worked hard and gave it everything I had in me.

It was a little awkward when the other students looked at me with questioning eyes, obviously wondering how I was going to play the drums with my short arms. But I was ready to show them my talent. The percussion director, Mr. Reese, lined us up and explained the process. He said that by the end of the day he would know who would stay and who would be cut. I had about seven hours to show him my stuff.

After we ran through a few of the pieces, my stomach did a flip-flop when I saw Mr. Reese walk over to talk to my mom. I thought, *Is he cutting me before I even have a chance to try out?* I was relieved when he came back and asked each of us to run through a few bars of music. *Whew. Deep breath.*

We broke for lunch, and I felt pretty good. Mom told me the drum teacher had asked her what I expected from the tryout. She told him I expected to be treated like the rest of the students. She said I'd dreamed of being in the Husky Marching Band since I was a fifth grader, but I didn't want any special treatment.

It seemed my mom was a nervous wreck all throughout the audition. She kept leaving to go for walks around the stadium to get rid of her nervous energy. When it came time for the end of the day wrap-up, I could tell by the look on her face that she was as scared as I was.

The teacher told the entire group to come back the next morning. *Yes! I made it through the first day.*

As we drove home, I imagined myself in the purple and gold uniform, marching into Husky Stadium to a cheering crowd of seventy-five thousand people. I could hear the screams of the fans. I could imagine the student Dawg Pack section of the stadium filled with fists pumping to the beat of the Husky fight song, "Bow Down to Washington."

Mom encouraged me to stay positive and hope for the best. We talked about the areas I struggled with, like flipping sticks or hard rim shots. I didn't think they were deal breakers, so I kept a positive attitude. It seemed so real to me. I just knew I'd make the squad.

The next morning, the routine started again with the group practicing cadence and rhythm routines. Then we had to show him our stuff individually. That part was scary. I could keep up with most of the beats, but I couldn't flip my sticks like the rest of the students. There were a few times I fell off the beat because my hands just couldn't move as fast as everyone else's.

I was frustrated and thought for sure I would get cut at the end of the day. So when he said to come back for another day, I was beside myself with excitement.

That night I said, "Mom, I think I'm going to make it! He said on Monday he would know by the end of the day who had what it took to make the squad. It's Tuesday night, and I haven't been cut yet. I think this is it! Can you believe it?"

"I sure hope so, Gabe. I don't know if I can take one more day of this tension. I wish he'd just make up his mind so we can get on with planning your freshman year."

The next day, Mom prayed with me before we got out of the van. She asked God to give us peace. We agreed that we trusted God no matter what the outcome would be. We blessed each of the other drummers and asked that the best squad would be chosen.

I saw the drum instructor talk to my mom a few times during the day. That made me really nervous. What was he saying? Then when I saw her crying after coming back from her walk, I had a sinking feeling that I was going to be cut. After lunch, I learned I was right.

Mr. Reese called my mom over and told us together that he had to cut me. With a precision routine like the Husky drumline performs, he didn't have room for the variations my sticking caused. He told me he admired me for auditioning but was sorry he couldn't see how it would work out.

I was crushed. We waited about half an hour for Dr. McDavid, the marching band director. He wanted to talk to me personally. He said he was sorry that I didn't make the band but felt it was the best decision for the drumline. He encouraged me by telling me he was impressed with my ability and suggested I try out for concert band.

I explained that I've always wanted to be in marching band, not concert band. I had a lump in my throat the size of a golf ball as I thanked him for the chance to try out.

After Mom loaded my wheelchair into the van, we both cried. It felt like déjà vu. The scene was the same as the day in kindergarten when I realized my arms and legs weren't going to grow. Disappointment hit me right in the gut. Realization of my limitations stared me in the face. This was one of the days that I really hated my disability.

I thought about how if only they had given me a chance to be part of the drumline, many people would have benefited from seeing how someone with a severe disability can still contribute to the marching band. But it wasn't part of the plan for my life.

I hung on to the disappointment for awhile. I have to admit that it was hard to get over. But I made the choice to move on and enjoy Husky football anyway. I bought season tickets so I could attend every game and cheer them on from the student section.

I am sharing this story with you in hope that you will see that even though sometimes things don't go your way, you can endure through the loss of a dream and move on from it with grace. The alternative is to hang on to the disappointment, which wastes precious days. I will never have this moment, this hour, or this day again. Why waste it living with discouragement?

MY MESSAGE IS C.L.E.A.R.

It isn't always easy to move from discouragement to joy, but God continues to fill my cup up when the disappointments of life drain it. I have to keep going back to Him in prayer and asking for more grace to get through the tough times. Life is so much easier when I choose joy.

Looking back, I believe that God had a plan to protect me during my freshman year of college, just like He protected me in high school. I realize that it would have been hard to keep up with my studies with the distraction of the marching band activities. Maybe God was simply protecting me from a major detour that would not have been the best for me. I eventually learned to reframe the way I viewed that disappointment by trusting that God had a better plan for me. I then asked Him for wisdom to know what I should do next.

I wish I could say that not being selected for marching band was the only difficult thing I endured at the University of Washington. But my sophomore year, I went through a different season of endurance.

I moved off campus into a nice apartment with my good friend. It was great to have my own place. By then I had my service dog, Ruth, and we had plenty of room for her to be there with me. Things were going well, but being further away from the main activities of the campus made it more difficult to participate in functions. I didn't have as many friends to hang out with, and I got lonely.

On my way to the grocery store one gray and cloudy afternoon, I noticed a girl standing across the street, talking on her cell phone. I figured she was just another pretty girl who would walk by without acknowledging my existence, but I was pleasantly surprised! She stopped to get my attention and waved at me with her phone at her ear. She looked me in the eye and smiled. I wondered if my smile was a dead giveaway that she had made my day.

I wanted to turn around and introduce myself to her, but I thought that would be a little awkward. I was definitely smiling all through the grocery store. That small, kind gesture made a bad day so much better.

Over the next couple of months, we kept running into each other on campus. We exchanged waves, but I never had a chance to meet her and find out her name.

My season ticket seats for Husky basketball were right above the student section and the tunnel entrance for the players and cheerleaders. At the next Husky game, this same girl waved at me in the tunnel as the players and cheerleaders entered the court. She was a University of Washington Husky cheerleader.

It was a couple of months later when I finally found her profile on Facebook®. We have a mutual friend who is also a cheerleader, so I recognized the girl's picture one day when I was on my other friend's Facebook® page. I learned that her name is Piper.

During my statistics class, I got up the guts to send her a Facebook friend request. (Yes, I confess I was on Facebook during class.) My phone vibrated about twenty minutes later with a nice message from her, along with her acceptance of my friend request. We became good friends over the next several months.

Piper has many of the C.L.E.A.R. qualities I speak of, and I truly appreciate our friendship. She had the courage to reach out and say "hi" to me on the street that day. That simple gesture really encouraged me. She has excellent leadership qualities and cares about the people in her life. She also has endured some of her own hard times at school, including the tragic death of one of her best friends. Piper's positive attitude shines brightly in her fun personality, and most of all, I like how she respects our friendship by taking time to meet for coffee, lunch, or a Mariner game. One time she even drove out of her way to pick me up for a Seattle Sounders soccer game. Her kindness and generosity have blessed me, and her friendship has helped me to endure.

MY MESSAGE IS C.L.E.A.R.

People like Piper are rare in my life. Not very many people reach out like she did. We are still good friends, and I really appreciate her. I hope you'll follow Piper's example and understand how a simple wave goes a long way to encourage another person. It might even develop into a friendship.

Slight Detour

During that same year, I spent more time with my roommate and less time doing my homework. If he didn't have class and wanted to go play soccer, I'd skip class just to have something to do with a friend. A volunteer provided by disability services took notes for me in my classes, so I thought I could read the notes and still learn what I had missed. But I started skipping more and more classes, which led to missing homework assignments and failing tests. I was doing things I shouldn't have been doing, and everything spiraled downhill.

At the end of the fall quarter, my heart pounded when I opened an e-mail from the University of Washington informing me that I was on academic probation. I didn't tell my mom and dad. When they asked how I was doing, I was dishonest and told them everything was going fine. I didn't ask for help from the many services available to me because I was too embarrassed to admit I was in trouble. I figured I could handle it on my own and work hard to get my grades up before anyone knew I was struggling.

It only got worse. By the end of the winter quarter, I received the bad news that I officially had been dropped from the University of Washington. My dream of graduating as a Washington Husky came to a screeching halt. I was devastated.

I moved out of my apartment and back home with my parents. All the independence I had worked for seemed to be ripped right out from under me because of my own dumb choices. I fell into a deep

E = ENDURANCE

sadness of embarrassment and disappointment, but my mom and dad supported me. They encouraged me to continue attending my City Church youth group. We also checked into the possibility of my getting back into the University of Washington, but my appeal was denied. Now what was I going to do?

Everyone in my family was asking me how college was going, and I needed to tell them what was up. I wrote an e-mail to my extended family, explaining what happened. It took great courage to type up that e-mail, but I'm glad I did. It was like a big load was lifted off my chest.

I received e-mail responses filled with encouraging words, reminding me to hang in there and keep working toward my goals. Everyone was very understanding, and it helped me deal with the disappointing situation.

Soon I applied to go to school at Cascadia Community College, which is near my house. The counseling center helped me figure out my transfer credits, and I registered for the next fall. I met with my Department of Vocational Rehab counselor, Francis, and he helped me decide the best path back to my goals. It felt good to be back on track.

I'll admit it is not always easy when you face your challenges like this, but I take it one day at a time. My goal is to be a full-time speaker, encouraging audiences all over the world. I believe with all of my heart that it is what God has called me to do. I'm working on building that ministry while I continue to take college classes. I will complete my Associates Degree in 2012, and then I'll see where God leads. I've learned that it is best to wait and listen for God's next move on this journey through life.

Is there something you are going through that seems to be taking forever? Are you struggling with a long-term illness or a hard situation at home or at school? Have you been disappointed by recent events? Has unemployment got you depressed? Hang in there. Endure. It will get better.

MY MESSAGE IS C.L.E.A.R.

Don't waste today worrying about tomorrow. Just take things one grace-filled day at a time. Each day you will gather new strength to get you through. And soon you will realize that you become stronger each time you move beyond difficult times. I'd be glad to help you endure whatever you are going through. E-mail me at Gabe@ GabesHOPE.org if you need encouragement during a difficult time.

E = ENDURANCE

Keeping in line with the drumline—WHS Marching Band, 2007 I loved Friday night football games when our high school marching band played during the game and performed on the field at halftime. The bracket to hold my snare drum sits on the front of my wheelchair. It was made by my friend Jeff Jones. He also moved my joy stick from my hand down to my foot. This allowed me to use both hands to drum. If you think walking and chewing gum at the same time is hard, try driving while playing the drums!

Endurance Challenge

- Try not to give up—never say never.
- Take one step at a time toward your goal.
- Trust that God has a good plan for your life.
- Treat every day as the most important day of your life.
- Think of ways to help others endure their hard times.

CHAPTER 9

A = ATTITUDE

Attitude: manner, disposition, feeling, position, etc., with regard to a person or thing; tendency or orientation, especially of the mind.[7]

Attitude isn't everything, but it is the main thing that affects everything.[8]

—*John Maxwell*

I ONCE HEARD a pastor share this thought: "You can determine your attitude, but your attitude determines your future." This has been true in my life. My mom tells me I've always had a good attitude, but we both know that there have been times when I wasn't so positive. However, I don't like to stay on the negative side of life; it stinks over there.

Your attitude is a choice, really. It's sort of like when you are looking at a glass of water that is filled up half way. You can choose to look at it two different ways. Do you consider the glass to be half full or half empty? I personally like to think of the glass as half full. It is a more positive approach. I don't know about you, but for me, people who always view things negatively are a drain on my energy.

Every day when I get up, I choose to have a good attitude. Sometimes it's hard to get out and face the world. Probably one of the most difficult things for me on a daily basis is the fact that there is rarely a day that someone doesn't stare at me. I mean bug-eyed, jaw-dropping stares that last a long time. I'm waiting for the day when someone who is staring at me walks into a lamp post and gets knocked out cold. Trust me when I say it has almost happened several times.

Sometimes kids pull their arms inside their T-shirt sleeves and try to imitate my short arms. Other days they might cover their mouth as they point at me. I've even made a few young kids cry. I'm not sure why, because I'm really not that scary.

Then there is one scenario I've experienced that is difficult for me to understand. Let's say I'm at the mall, and a young boy notices me and my wheelchair. He tugs on his mom's shirt, points, and says, "Mommy, what is wrong with that boy?"

Rather than simply answering his question, the mom freaks out, grabs his hand, and jerks him down the hall. Then I watch as he looks back at me, crying because she scared him so bad when she freaked out. He only wanted her to answer his curious question. Now he is scared to death of people who look different because it was such a negative encounter.

I've even seen kids get spanked by their parents for asking about me. It would be so much better if the parents would let the children come over and ask me questions. Then we could chat for a minute. (Please respect my time and personal space and don't ask me a million questions. One or two will do.) Then that young boy or girl would understand that people with disabilities are not scary. Everybody wins.

Other times I've had kids point and say, "You look really weird with short arms." Their parents watch out of the corner of an eye, pretending they didn't hear or see what happened. Then they walk ahead of the child and let him or her continue making ugly remarks.

MY MESSAGE IS C.L.E.A.R.

Nobody wins in that scenario.

I wish parents and grandparents would not ignore these curious questions. Young people (and some old people too, unfortunately) need to be taught respect for people's differences. It would be so much better to use situations like these as teaching moments to help children understand that the world is full of people who are different in one way or another. Being different is not wrong; it's just different.

One Mother's Day a few years ago, we were at a restaurant eating lunch. I must have looked scary to a four- or five-year-old kid who sat across from us. After poking his head around his chair and checking me out about a hundred times, he popped up over the top of his chair and said, "Hey, your arms are short. You look like a Tyrannosaurus Rex." Then he looked over at his mom and said, "Is that boy a T-Rex, Mommy?"

That remark was a first for me. A T-Rex? What a scary thought! I had to admit that when you look at me from a side profile, I do sort of resemble a T-Rex. You get the picture, bent legs and short arms.

His mom about died right there on the spot from embarrassment. She explained to him that I was not a T-Rex. She was trying to pull his attention away from me and apologized several times about his remarks. But I simply introduced myself and asked him to come over to our table to check out the horn on my wheelchair. Then I explained that I was born with short arms and bent legs. I showed the little guy that I don't have the same gnarly teeth as a T-Rex dinosaur, and I promised him that I wasn't planning on eating him for lunch.

We sat and chatted for awhile and became fast friends. He realized I was not so freaky, and I thought he was really cute. I appreciated how his parents let him come over to our table to talk to me. I don't mind answering questions because it educates everyone about people like me. It also helps them to see that even though I might look different, I'm really not that different.

A = ATTITUDE

In elementary school, I went into each classroom at the beginning of the year to show the students my wheelchair and answer their questions about my life. Once we addressed their curious imaginations with the truth about my disability, the staring and finger-pointing stopped.

I will admit that dealing with staring kids is really hard. I don't see myself as being that different, but people seem to get a bit freaked out when they see me for the first time. They let fear win and usually don't approach me. They never get the chance to realize that I'm a pretty normal guy.

Fear is an attitude I'd like to see people overcome. Dealing with this issue could cause me to have a negative attitude, but what's the point of choosing to see it negatively? It really doesn't get me anywhere. It is something I can't control. I've chosen to deal only with the things I can control.

Sometimes kids are just plain mean. But I can't change them, I can only adjust my response to what they say or do. I choose to believe they mean no harm. They just don't know me yet and have not been taught proper respect.

This choice of a better attitude toward people who stare didn't happen overnight. Earlier in my life, I had a few stare-downs with kids at the mall. I wanted them to see what it was like to have glaring eyes looking at them, so I chose to retaliate by staring right back with one of those looks that said, *I'd really like to run you over with my wheelchair right about now*. But that only invoked more fear in the kids and didn't accomplish anything positive.

My parents and I sat down and talked about the situation. They helped me to realize that people point and stare because they are curious. Most likely, they have never seen someone with a body like mine. No one has taken the time to teach them about respecting people's differences and being polite when they look at me.

MY MESSAGE IS C.L.E.A.R.

My attitude toward others is in my control, and I've come to experience that a positive attitude goes a long way. I've always tried to approach the difficult things with a gentle smile and a kind word rather than trying to fight back.

When I was in second grade, each day my dad parted my hair and combed it neatly to the side. It helped keep my thick curls in place. After I got to school, a boy in my class would come up to me and rub his hands over my hair to make it stand up all afro-like. Sometimes he made me look like a clown. Then he would run away.

My arms don't reach the top of my head, so I can't fix my hair if it gets messed up. But even if I could have fixed it, I didn't like how he invaded my space. It was rude. He thought it was funny. I kept asking him to stop, but day after day, he kept messing my hair up. It really ticked me off. There were some days when I was very tempted to run him over with my wheelchair, but I made a different choice. I chose to use my voice.

I talked to my brother and my parents about what was going on. We prayed about what to do. My parents taught me how to handle the situation by letting the kid know I didn't appreciate what he was doing to me. I learned to speak up for myself, but not in a mean way. I learned to express myself in a way that helped him understand that I didn't like being picked on.

Before I talked to my parents, each day when the boy messed with my hair, I would say, *"Stop it!"* He didn't listen, and he ran away. Then I sat there feeling powerless. Inside I was steaming mad. My parents and I decided that rather than telling him to stop, I should take a little different approach. My dad practiced with me, teaching me to use the biggest voice I could muster up.

The next day, I was out on the playground, and I could see this kid headed my way. I looked up and said a prayer, "Okay, God, it's you and me against this bully. Help me get him to stop messing up my hair."

the kid reached toward my head, I screamed at the top of "Hey! Keep your hands *off* my head."

He was so shocked at my loud voice that he pulled his hand back and stared at me with tear-filled eyes. He said, "Gosh, Gabe, you don't have to *yell* at me. Okay, I won't touch you again, all right?"

"Thank you. I appreciate you keeping your hands to yourself." I wheeled away with a smile because I had found a way to speak up for myself. He never touched my hair again. I learned that I could handle the situation in a positive manner, and no one got their toes run over by my chair. I think we were both happy with the outcome, because a one-hundred-and-fifty pound wheelchair would really smash your toes.

A positive approach is always best. Sometimes you have to experiment with ways to get your point across, but it is worth it to be upbeat.

Over the years I've met some incredible people who choose to have a positive attitude in the midst of life's adversities. I have learned from their example and want to share some of their stories with you.

Nick Vujicic

A hero is defined as someone who gives his life for something bigger than himself. Once you get to know him, you'll understand why Nick Vujicic is my hero. I met him several years ago at a church in Richland, Washington. He was the keynote speaker for a youth event. My dad arranged for me to meet him.

When we went through the buffet line to load our plates for dinner at this event, Nick invited me to sit at his table. We hit it off right away and talked all through the meal. It was great hanging out with someone who could relate to my life.

Nick was born with no arms and no legs. Just like my parents, his parents had no idea of the cause of his birth defects. When he was a young boy, he also went through a hard time dealing with the difficulty of having such a limited body. He didn't like being different either, and he prayed for God to give him arms and legs.

Before long, he chose to believe that although he didn't get a miracle of receiving arms and legs, he could be a miracle to help change lives by ministering to people and sharing the gift of his positive attitude. He knew he could help others understand that each person is a special gift sent to earth to do something great.

Nick travels the world, speaking to countless schools, churches, prisons, orphanages, hospitals, and stadiums, sharing his life-changing message of hope. He is funny and entertains audiences with stories explaining how he has chosen to laugh at his circumstances. He also believes that because of his positive outlook on life, he is being used as the hands and feet of God to spread the message of hope throughout the world.

One of my favorite things about Nick is that he gives the best hugs. Yes, even with no arms, he hugs with an intensity that warms your heart. Great hugs come from a heart of unconditional love. He looks you straight in the eye and listens during your conversations. He makes you feel like you are the most important person in that moment. These qualities come from the confidence he has in knowing that God has a plan and purpose to use him mightily. He is willing to do what it takes to bring joy to those around him. He truly inspires me.

Nick feels his life is limitless. He started a nonprofit organization called Life Without Limbs. I hope you will visit his website at http://www.LifeWithoutLimbs.org and learn about his amazing ministry throughout the world. I also recommend his book *Life Without Limits*.

There is a link to Nick's website and book on our Gabriel's Foundation of HOPE website, http://www.GabesHOPE.org. I've also listed contact information at the end of this book in the helpful resources section. I encourage you to check out his amazing ministry.

People like Nick inspire me to maintain a positive attitude. Although I have dipped down to a negative attitude on occasion, I don't stay there for long. I have realized that being negative does not serve me well. I have learned to understand that all things work together for good, and if I simply trust God with my life, it will all work out in the end.

I would be lying if I didn't say that some days are hard. But I make a conscious choice. My mom calls it the choice to rejoice.

I can tell you from experience that living with a positive attitude is much more fun than living in negativity.

Have you ever been around a person who is negative? It's really hard to be around them for any length of time. They complain about everything from the weather to the price of gas to the color of the sky. I just don't understand what good it does to focus on the negative things around me.

So let's make a choice to rejoice together. There are too many people in this world who need us to point them to hope. Your attitude can help change someone's life.

Tomorrow morning I want you to look at yourself in the mirror and see a person with an incredible future. Trust that God has a future for you that is full of hope (Jeremiah 29:11). Remind yourself of this truth by using my favorite Bible verse: "I can do all things through Christ who strengthens me." (Philippians 4:13) NKJV.

Now that's the kind of attitude I'm talking about! I hope you will go through life with a positive attitude.

My Baseball Story

One thing that has helped me maintain a positive attitude is my participation in sports activities. Zane is an athlete. I loved watching him play sports, starting with T-ball when he was five and I was two. A few of his coaches let me sit in the dugout because they usually won when I was hanging with the boys. They called me their "lucky charm."

I always wanted to play baseball but never dreamed I could bat with my short arms. Then my mom and dad found out about Challenger Little League. The Challenger Division was established in 1992 as a separate part of Washington State District Eight Little League. This league allows boys and girls with physical and mental challenges to enjoy the game of baseball along with the millions of other children who participate in this sport worldwide.

We learned that Gary and Bev Newsome had started a league in our area, with two teams available in my home town. I was counting the days until my sixth birthday, when I became eligible to play.

I remember the day of my first practice like it was yesterday. We went to Target and bought a left-handed glove and a plastic bat for me before heading for the field.

When mom pulled up to the field, there was only one other player waiting for the coach. My mom told me she was a little nervous because she wasn't even sure if they let people in wheelchairs play in this league. But that worry went away the moment she opened the van door. A girl named Laura gave me a warm welcome.

"Hey, is he one of our new players?" Laura asked as she walked up to our van.

"Is this where the Blue Jays practice? My son Gabe is joining that team," Mom answered.

Laura leaned into the van window. "You're in the right place. My name is Laura, and I play Challenger baseball too. Does your son walk or use a wheelchair?"

Mom opened the back door and pulled out the ramps. "He drives a wheelchair."

A = ATTITUDE

"Cool. It's nice to meet you, Gabe." Laura patted me on the shoulder. "Welcome to the Blue Jays. We need more wheelchairs." Then she skipped off into the outfield.

I have loved every minute of Challenger League Baseball. Since that first season, we've grown to have four teams in Woodinville. Many of the kids on my team have been with us from the beginning. We play two innings each game. Everyone bats. Everyone gets on base. Everyone plays in the outfield. Everyone has a blast. My dad has coached me for fifteen years and is always recruiting more players.

I don't sit in my wheelchair to bat because my chair is too confining. I use a rubber ball and a smaller aluminum bat, and I wear a protective shoe that Chick's Shoes of Mercer Island (http://www.chicks-shoes.com/) custom-made to protect my knee from the rocks on the field. My dad or my brother will pitch the ball to me, and then I hop around the bases on my butt. That can get pretty tiring, especially when I hit a home run and have to run all the bases.

My senior year of high school we had a jamboree where all the teams in the Seattle area joined together for a round-robin tournament and barbecue picnic. My whole family was in town because it was the week of my graduation. It was wonderful to have so many people see me play.

That Saturday jamboree went down in my history book as an epic day. With my whole family watching, Zane pitched one low and inside. Right before he threw the ball, I said, "This one's going out." I'd almost hit it out of the ball park before, but usually the ball bounced just before the fence. This time, Zane threw the ball, and I swung the bat with everything in me. My cousins and aunts and uncles were on their feet watching as it soured out of the park. *Home run!* I couldn't believe it. I bounced around the bases to the cheers (and tears) of my huge family. That was truly a day I'll never forget.

All of the people on my baseball team have incredible attitudes.

MY MESSAGE IS C.L.E.A.R.

They each have their own story of what disability qualifies them to play Challenger baseball. For two hours every Saturday in the spring, we're just a bunch of kids who love to play baseball.

Come out and see us sometime. I believe you won't be disappointed. Many people who have come to watch have shed a few tears. One thing is for sure, if you need a change in attitude, Challenger Little League Baseball will surely change your perspective on life! Check out the resource page in the back of my book for more information on how to find a Challenger team in your area.

I hope these stories of people with great attitudes have inspired you to check your attitude meter. Is it positive? I sure hope so.

A = ATTITUDE

Hanging out at lunch with my hero Nick Vujicic He lives a C.L.E.A.R. life,
even though he was born with no arms or legs!
His attitude inspires me to live with no limits.

Aiming for the fence. I hit my first home run at a Challenger
Little League Jamboree with my family cheering me on.

Attitude Challenge

- Determine your attitude, and your attitude determines your future.
- Don't be negative; it doesn't look good on you.
- During hard times, make a choice to rejoice.
- Don't be disabled with a bad attitude.
- Day by day, trust that God will give you strength.

CHAPTER 10

R = RESPECT

Respect: esteem for or a sense of the worth or excellence of a person, a personal quality or ability; the condition of being esteemed or honored: to be held in respect.[9]

Respect for the fragility and importance of an individual life is still the mark of an educated man.[10]

—*Norman Cousins*

THE FINAL LETTER in the word C.L.E.A.R. is "R," and it stands for "respect." It is an attitude or feeling toward something. Another word for respect is "honor." Please respect and honor the people in your life. This list includes your parents, siblings, friends, teachers, bosses, and government officials.

We should also respect the law and general rules of conduct at school, work, or play. For instance, a good driver will respect the speed limit. When we respect something, we don't violate a boundary. Like when my parents ask me to be home at midnight, I respect that boundary and come home before the requested time.

I think you should also respect your stuff, including cell phones, cars, toys, games, and your home—especially your bedroom. If I disrespect the things I have, I'm probably not going to get them replaced. It is just the way it works. When you take care of the little things, you end up being responsible enough to handle more. So I choose respect.

My family has helped me to understand the importance of respecting authority. I trust that people with authority in my life are there to help make my life easier. So it has never been difficult for me to respect them. If my mom asks me to clean up my mess, I do it.

Most parents try hard to do the best job in raising their kids. However, sometimes they make mistakes, so please give them a break. But if anyone is harming you in any way, please tell someone, and get help to resolve the issue. Don't hide the truth. Respect yourself enough to stop any abusive behavior.

Please respect your siblings. It makes me very sad to watch brothers and sisters pick on each other. My brother and I have always treated each other with love, kindness, and respect.

During your school years, you spend a lot of time with your teachers. I hope you respect them. If your teachers ask you to turn in an assignment, honor their authority, and follow their request. If you don't, you will have to pay the consequences. I've learned that the hard way.

Newsflash! Contrary to some students' beliefs, your teachers are not out to get you. They do not come to work every day to make your life miserable. They work hard to give you an education so that you can go change the world.

Occasionally, there might be a teacher with a bad attitude who takes it out on his or her students. That's not right, and I hope there are principals out there who will do something about that negative behavior. But for the most part, teachers work very hard to educate their students for a better life. Unfortunately, sometimes they don't get much respect.

Maybe you can lead the way of respect in your home and at your school or job. Be respectful, and earn the respect of others.

MY MESSAGE IS C.L.E.A.R.

I've noticed that people who don't respect others often have little self-respect. For whatever reason, they don't think very highly of themselves, so they choose to treat others with disrespect. That kind of thinking just does not compute in my brain. I don't see the point.

Now I know from experience that one of the hardest things in life is peer pressure. No matter how old you are, peer pressure exists. Maybe it's pressure from a coworker or a fellow student or a family member. No matter who you are, you have to learn to respond properly and respectfully. If the person applying the pressure is asking you to do something you don't agree with or if they want you to be someone different than your true self, don't do it. I've watched too many of my friends go against their moral compass while trying to get someone to like them or to be part of the "in" crowd. I fell into that trap and lived to regret it. It's really not worth it in the end. Respect yourself enough to say "no."

Guys: This message is for you. I feel I can't talk about respect without bringing this up. Please value the girls in your life. Treat them with gentleness and kindness. I know too many stories of girls who have felt disrespected by guys. Be a leader, and show them respect.

In addition to respecting laws, authority, your stuff, and others, you need to respect yourself. This is critical to the success of life. We have only one chance in the body God gave us. Therefore, we need to take care of it by exercising, eating healthy food, and not putting ugly chemicals like alcohol and drugs into it. We need to learn to say "no" when friends use peer pressure to ask us to do things that hurt the only body we've got.

One thing that drives me crazy is when people don't respect my abilities. This happened to me several times in high school, especially when we had group projects. We divided up the work on the project, and I was fully capable of completing my part of the assignment. But more times than not, one of the team members would take over my part and tell me they had it covered. Then they wouldn't return my calls when we tried to arrange for the group to get together. They finished the project without me, and I had to live with the grade, even though I didn't have any input. It was frustrating, and I felt disrespected.

I brought the issue up to the group and my teacher. I was surprised to learn that they all thought they were helping me by doing my work. I used my voice to let them know I wanted to do my own work.

Please give people a chance to use their gifts and talents rather than making the assumption that they are not capable. I think you might be surprised at the abilities that shine through when someone is given a chance.

I also hope you will respect the differences of your peers. Everyone has individual preferences for hairstyles and clothes. My heart aches when I listen to people making fun of other people for the way they look—not only when they make fun of a body like mine but also when they make fun of people's choices to color their hair or wear certain clothes.

Let's respect the unique qualities of every individual we encounter. We may not agree with people's choices to get a tattoo or wear a rainbow-colored mohawk or pierce their nose, but we can still respect them. God created each one of us in a unique and awesome fashion. Celebrate your peers. Don't make fun of them.

Another issue I have to deal with is the lack of respect people have for disabled parking spaces. Please help me here. I need the space to get my wheelchair safely out of the van. Almost everywhere I go, someone parks in a disabled space without the legal parking permit hanging in the car. I want to scream sometimes at the insensitivity of the drivers who violate this code.

We had two disabled spaces near the gym at my elementary school. I lost count of how many times people parked in the disabled spaces without a parking permit on their car. It was usually when Mom picked me up from my after-school program. She was forced to park down the road, where there was no way for me to get off the sidewalk and onto the street. I had to use the disabled ramp on the sidewalk right outside the gym and then drive down the road while dodging cars to get to the van. Several times we did this routine in the pouring rain.

One time my mom went into the gym to ask the other moms to move their illegally parked cars. Rather than complying with the request, one woman told Mom she felt sorry for her because of my disability. I wish she would have been sorry she had parked illegally! She said she didn't think there were any disabled people around at that time of the day so she thought it was okay to park in that space.

People! The notice posted near the disabled parking spaces does not have a time frame on it. It does not say, "It is okay to park here if you think there are no disabled people around." It does not say, "It is okay to park here if you are just running into the bank to get some cash." It does not say, "I know it is too far to walk from the available space at Costco®, so please use the disabled space for your convenience." It does not say, "If you are a delivery truck, you can park here to make your deliveries." It clearly states: HANDICAPPED PARKING—STATE PERMIT REQUIRED or something of that nature. And did you know that the fine for parking in a disabled space without a permit is between $100.00 and $250.00, depending on where you live?

I hope you are willing to help those of us with disabilities by honoring the disabled parking spaces. And please don't use your grandma's disability permit to park closer or to take advantage of the free parking for people with disabilities. I think that is just plain rude, not to mention dishonest.

I've been dealing with this for as long as we've had our disabled parking permit. It's a difficult battle to fight. Lately, we've been taking photos of the illegally parked cars and posting them on Facebook®. Then we report the license plate number to local authorities. We also log the cars in at a website created to report fraudulent use of disabled parking spaces. There is a website at http://www.handicappedfraud. org that allows you to track the license plates and location of violators. Some county police departments follow this website and take action on the reported violations. There is even an app for your phone to allow you to report a violator on the spot. I like that!

Check our Gabriel's Foundation of HOPE website at http://www. GabesHOPE.org for information on stickers to place on the cars of those who violate the laws about disabled parking spaces. It helps to increase awareness that violators are noticed.

Whew! Disabled parking is a sensitive subject for me. Thank you for being respectful in this area of my life. Together we can make a difference.

Another area of respect I'd like to talk more about is bullying. Bullying can be both physical and emotional and takes on many different forms, including name-calling, hitting, threatening others, teasing, kicking, spreading rumors, sending mean e-mails, or purposefully excluding someone from an activity. None of this is much fun for those being bullied.

I don't understand the purpose of bullying. When I see someone being mean to someone else, I want to say, "Really? Are you serious, Mr. Bully?"

My mom always says that hurt people hurt people. Usually those mean kids are hurting inside. We have decided that the best thing we can do is to pray for those hurting people so that they will stop hurting others.

Please join me in a zero tolerance level toward bullying. Speak up. Tell a teacher. Tell your boss if it is happening at your office. Don't ignore what you see happening around you. Every person has value and should never be bullied. I think it's awesome how each one of us is so uniquely different. All of our differences have a purpose behind them, and I believe God has a plan for every single human being.

Remember, when you bully someone, you are bullying one of God's treasures. He doesn't like it. Neither do I. Neither does the person on the other end of those mean words or deeds.

Do you believe you are a treasure? I do. And I believe you are a treasure worthy of respect. According to the Bible, God thinks so too.

> For you are a holy people to the LORD your God; the LORD your God has chosen you to be a people for Himself, a special treasure above all the peoples on the face of the earth.
>
> —Deuteronomy 7:6 NKJV

> Don't be bluffed into silence by the threats of bullies. There's nothing they can do to your soul, your core being. Save your fear for God, who holds your entire life—body and soul—in his hands. Forget about yourself.
>
> What's the price of a pet canary? Some loose change, right? And God cares what happens to it even more than you do. He pays even greater attention to you, down to the last detail—even numbering the hairs on your head! So don't be intimidated by all this bully talk. You're worth more than a million canaries.
>
> —Matthew 10:28–31 MSG

So I'm here to challenge every reader of this book to consider respect as an important part of life. The person you see every day in the mirror is a treasure and worthy of respect. Don't believe anyone who tries to tell you otherwise. Just be the best that God created you to be. Don't try to fit into someone else's shoes. You'll just end up with sore feet as you walk along a detour from the best path for your l·

R = RESPECT

If you are being bullied, or if someone is mistreating you, I am so sorry. That is not right. I hope you realize that God sees your pain. The Bible says in Psalm 56:8 that He even puts your tears in a bottle. Also, please don't let your anger cause you to bully back. Revenge isn't good either. Tell an adult. Don't wait to get help to resolve the situation.

More importantly, remember what God says about you. Forget what those mean people say. They don't know what they are talking about. God says you are wonderfully made. You are a treasure. He has a plan for you, and it is good. Your future looks bright when you focus on what God says.

I have great respect for every player in the
Challenger Baseball League. This is a photo of the members of the
Woodinville Challenger Blue Jays.
Front (L–R): Sean, Kobey, Rosie, Ryan M., Ryan D., Coach Steve, Nick
Second Row (L–R): Me, Dean, Daniel, Nathan
Back Row (L–R): Coach Rick, Paul, Jason, Doug, Trenton, Luke.

Respect Challenge

- Respect yourself by taking care of your body.
- Respect your stuff.
- Respect your authorities.
- Respect people's differences.
- Respect disabled parking spaces.

CHAPTER 11

MY HOPE AND MY STRENGTH

Hope: To feel that something desired may happen; to look forward to with desire and reasonable confidence; to believe, desire, or trust.[11]

Learn from yesterday, live for today, hope for tomorrow.[12]
> —*Albert Einstein*

Optimism is the faith that leads to achievement. Nothing can be done without hope.[13]
> —*Helen Keller*

MY WHOLE LIFE has been built on a foundation of hope. From the time I was born, my family has helped me to see a hope-filled future. Hope gets me through the tough times. I have something to look forward to when I can hope for a better tomorrow. And God gives me the ability and grace to keep hoping.

When I was born, my mom and dad weren't sure what to do. They didn't expect to have a son born with arms and legs that don't work properly. But that didn't stop them from loving me unconditionally and hoping for the best. Their foundation is strong because of Jesus and the amazing community of people in our family and our church.

I've been a part of a church for as long as I can remember. My parents told me we started consistently attending Eastside Foursquare Church when I was two years old. The thing I remember most from that time in my life is the climbing toys in our Sunday school classroom. I could play on these toys without getting muddy. And we usually ate Goldfish crackers for our snack. I still love Goldfish crackers. I also liked the fact that there was an elevator in the church.

My dad helped out in my Sunday school class, and we had a lot of fun. Mom usually volunteered in Zane's class. We attended all of the church camps and functions, and Mom and Dad were involved in a home fellowship group with several families.

While I was growing up, I had pastors come alongside me to encourage me to live for God. Our junior high pastor, Chris Peppler, spent an entire college quarter meeting with me once a week. We molded a chess set out of clay and made the board out of tiles. Each time we got together, he shared more about Jesus with me. This community of believers helped to make me strong.

When I was about eight or nine years old, I discovered a Bible verse that I knew was just for me. It was on a card my dad had taped on the mirror in our bathroom. On it, there was a photo of an extreme skier flying off a big jump, and the verse on the front of the card read, "I can do all this through Christ who strengthens me." I noticed next to the verse that it said Philippians 4:13. That 4:13 stuck out for me because I realized it matched my 4-13-90 birthday. I couldn't believe it. What a perfect message for a guy like me.

Philippians 4:13 has been my favorite verse ever since. I've used it often to help me realize that I can't do this on my own. I really need help. I need the help of my parents and my friends, but more importantly, I need the help of Jesus Christ, my Lord and Savior. I know that when I call on God, He will give me strength to get through my hard times.

The Bible tells me in Proverbs 18:24 (NKJV), "A man who has friends must himself be friendly, but there is a friend who sticks closer than a brother." To me, that friend is Jesus. Knowing that I always have Jesus helps me on days when I feel alone. I've learned through reading the Bible that it also tells me that Jesus will never leave me or forsake me (Hebrews 13:5). I don't think I could find a friend better than that.

This hope I found is something I want to pass along to other people. It has been my strong foundation. When we started our nonprofit organization in 2007, we named it Gabriel's Foundation of HOPE because hope keeps me persevering through my challenges. We also broke down the word "hope" into four letters that help explain what our organization is about.

"H" stands for *Help*. This is the definition of "help": "to give or provide what is necessary to accomplish a task or satisfy a need; contribute strength or means to; render assistance to; cooperate effectively with; aid; assist."[14] Our family realizes that living with a disability is not easy. It is our goal to help families and individuals who deal with a disability by providing financial support, resource information, and encouragement.

"O" stands for *Overcome*, which is defined as follows: "to get the better of in a struggle or conflict; conquer; defeat: to overcome the enemy; to gain the victory; win; conquer."[15] At one time or another, we face things we must overcome. But people living with a disability often have to overcome huge obstacles. Gabriel's Foundation of HOPE wants to find ways to help people overcome whatever obstacles they face. We use my speaking engagements as a source of encouragement to show people that if I can overcome my challenges, they can too. The funds we raise from doing these speaking engagements help finance the other areas of our ministry.

"P" stands for *Persevere*. Here is how one source defines "perseverance": "to persist in anything undertaken; maintain a purpose in spite of difficulty, obstacles, or discouragement; continue steadfastly; to bolster, sustain or uphold."[16] I believe persev the key to my successful life. I have made the decision that I will never give up. Can I just say that I owned the saying "Never say never" long before Justin Bieber was out of elementary school? With this positive and persevering attitude, I can maintain my purpose even when life is difficult.

I want to walk alongside others and help them to persevere too. We have found that simply knowing someone who relates to your challenges will give you courage to persevere. When there is hope on the horizon, it is easier to get through any storm. We want our nonprofit organization, Gabriel's Foundation of HOPE, to be that beacon of hope.

"E" stands for *Encourage*, which is defined as: "to inspire with courage, spirit, or confidence; to promote, advance, or prosper."[17] This encouragement goal of our foundation is my mom's favorite. I often see her sitting at our kitchen counter with a cup of tea, her pen, and a card. Mom writes notes to people who need to know someone cares. It's something you have to be intentional about.

Occasionally we'll get a call from Children's Hospital, asking us to pay a visit to someone who needs to be encouraged as they face life with a disability. We've met some incredible people through Children's Hospital.

I hope you will let us know if there is someone in your life who needs encouragement from Gabriel's Foundation of HOPE. It is amazing what a card, an e-mail, or a Facebook® post will do for someone who's feeling down and out.

Please check out the section on our website where you can order an encouragement card. We will send it to someone you love. Let us help you make someone's day a little brighter.

How about you? Where do you get your hope and strength? Do you have a community of people to help you through the difficult times? I highly recommend getting involved in a community group where friends will keep you accountable and encourage you daily.

MY MESSAGE IS C.L.E.A.R.

Do you know that God loves you? He wants the best for you, and I'd like to be an instrument of God's love by encouraging you when you need to build your hope and strength. Feel free to e-mail me at Gabe@GabesHOPE.org. I'd be glad to point you in the right direction.

This is the logo for our nonprofit organization Gabriel's Foundation of HOPE. Our goal is to bring hope to the world by helping individuals and families who live with disabilities. We encourage them to overcome and persevere through their challenges.

CHAPTER 12

MY FUTURE

I'M EXCITED ABOUT my future. It is filled with hope. My immediate goal is to finish school and get a full-time job. I want to work in a field where I can help people—social work or education or public speaking. I'm working on a degree in social work.

My dream is to continue to speak to thousands of people who would benefit from hearing my C.L.E.A.R. message of hope. If I could speak as a full-time job, I'd be a happy guy. I like speaking to a variety of different audiences.

If you'd like me to speak at a corporate event, I enjoy sharing stories with co-workers who might need encouragement or a change in perspective. I can speak to a specific topic or theme and enjoy interacting with people of all ages.

I often speak to entire schools in an assembly format, or I can break it up into individual classroom talks. I like the assembly format because there is a lot of synergy between me and the students. It really gets my energy pumping. I love it!

Whether you have a youth group event or would like me to speak to the whole congregation, I enjoy the opportunity to share my story in churches or at camps. I want to encourage people to walk in their gifts and purpose.

I hope to get married and have children someday. I continue to pray that God will bring me the woman he designed just for me. I know she's out there, and I wait patiently (practicing endurance), listening for God's voice to tell me she's the one.

My future plans also include owning a vehicle I can drive. Since I experienced what it is like to drive a car, it makes me want to get one all the more. I look forward to the freedom of being able to get to places without taking the bus or asking my parents to drive me.

Although I could buy a fairly nice car for the price of my wheelchair, I'm praying for an accessible car or van that is totally equipped just for me. I hope I don't have a gray hair by the time we save up to reach the $100,000 cost of the vehicle. I often visualize what it will be like when I have the kind of independence that driving will give me.

Because of my hope in God's good plan for me, I definitely see that vehicle in my future. Life's too short to spend my time waiting for tomorrow. In the meantime, I'll just make the best of today while I pray for my car or van.

I know my future is secure. Whatever happens to me here on earth, I am assured that I will spend eternity in heaven. God promises me this in the Gospels of the Bible. God sent His only Son, Jesus, to pay the ultimate price on the cross for my sin. He paid so I don't have to. I am thankful for this gift of salvation.

One of the most wonderful things about heaven is that I'll get a new body when I get there. I can't wait to experience what it is like to have long arms and legs. I imagine myself about six feet, five inches, with buff arms and legs. Now that's what I'm talking about! Can you imagine playing a game of pickup basketball with Jesus? Ha! That would be cool.

Yes, I look forward to heaven. But while I'm still here on earth, I plan to live the best life I can as I continue to share my C.L.E.A.R. message around the world. I will raise money for our foundation so we can continue to provide financial assistance and encouragement to the thousands of families who are affected by the disability of a family member.

I believe that God will continue to show me how to live out the purpose He has determined for my life. So I stay close to Him and keep listening for the next step. I'm sure He will make it C.L.E.A.R.

Here I am speaking at Fife High School. I share my stories with schools, businesses, community organizations, and churches.

MY FUTURE

My dad started the first leg of our hike up Mt. Rainier. It took us six hours
to get to Camp Muir and four hours to get back to the parking lot.
We were still smiling at the end.

Skiing with my family at Big Sky, Montana.
Check out the apple-crate snowboard.

CHAPTER 13

MY MOM AND DAD'S MESSAGE

Mom's Turn

IT HAS TRULY been an amazing journey raising two sons. They are equally incredible men. Zane was three years old when Gabe was born. Zane was convinced he was going to have a sister. Since everything felt so different in my pregnancy, I thought I was having a girl too. We were very excited for our second baby to arrive. I had no complications and felt really good the entire nine months.

A week before Gabe was born, I had an ultrasound to determine his position because my doctor thought he was breech (feet first). They were looking for the position of his head. If the technician saw something wrong with Gabe's arms or legs, she didn't tell me. What would I have done if I knew at that time? I probably would have lost sleep worrying over something I couldn't change. I'm thankful I didn't know until I saw his beautiful face.

As you can imagine, we were in shock when we first laid eyes on him. But it didn't take us long to realize that this incredible baby was a gift God sent to change our world. We immediately fell in love with his beautiful eyes and sweet spirit. He had the cutest chubby cheeks, a red nose, and a tiny chin. Any woman would kill for his beautiful eyelashes. He was snuggly too, and I loved that.

MY MOM AND DAD'S MESSAGE

Truly understanding that God has a good plan for us has been the most important part of raising Gabe. We don't focus on his disability. Instead, we encourage him to trust that God's plan for him is good. We know he will find a way to succeed.

Our friends and family played a significant role in helping to develop Gabe's healthy self-esteem. From the day he was born, he felt loved and accepted by many people who vowed to help him live a successful life.

In the months after Gabe was born, our future was uncertain. But there was a knowing in my heart that God would give us the grace to walk through a life that was very different than we had planned. From the beginning, I always believed that our sons came into this world to be used by God to make a difference in people's lives. I pray for them every day to hear God's voice as He directs them toward the best plan for their future.

Motherhood has been the biggest blessing of my life. I absolutely love it! Zane has taught me so many wise things as I've watched him become a young man. Gabe helped me to shift my priorities from my career to my family. In the few years it took for me to see the need for this change, I drew closer to God and realized His purpose for our lives.

It has been fun watching God's plan develop over the years, and we know we will continue to be used to touch the lives of other people. In this season, we see the speaking engagements to schools, businesses, community organizations, church congregations, and youth groups as one of our main assignments. We also know we'll be able to help other families starting down the path we've already traveled.

We are often called upon to meet with families who have children born with significant congenital birth defects. I tell them that I truly believe if God gave me the ability to choose Gabe's design, I would not change a thing about him. I must admit that for Gabe's sake, I would love things to be easier for him. Yet, I believe God is using him in the most profitable way for such a time as this.

In the Bible, the angel Gabriel was a messenger. Our Gabe has been a messenger of hope for my family and me. And now that he speaks to thousands of people every year, he is a messenger of hope for many. He has challenged me time and time again to look beyond my circumstances and see the potential in what seems to be impossible.

As son and mom, Gabe and I continue to learn how to handle the difficult times together. There have been days when I've had no idea how to help him deal with his struggles but have trusted God to show us the way. Recently God took me full circle and reminded me how He indeed works our difficult things for good.

I was on a two-day writing retreat at Camp Berachah in the Auburn-Black Diamond area of Washington State. My plan was to enter the final edits of this book and enjoy some quiet time. When I arrived, I was given a tour of the grounds. As I walked the path past the cabins, the pool, the dining hall, and the chapel, my mind was flooded with memories of the week Gabe attended his first summer church camp at that facility. That was eleven years ago, but it felt like yesterday as emotions I hadn't felt in years rose in my heart.

The summer of his fifth grade year, he spent a wonderful week at Camp Berachah, but it was one of the times Gabe was reminded of his limitations. We were not prepared for the disappointment he experienced when he couldn't climb on the climbing wall. He was sad when he was unable to participate in the obstacle course. Many of the games we played in the gymnasium were too difficult for him. And we had to figure out how I could help him in the boy's bathroom without embarrassing him or the other campers.

At the end of each day, I had to help him get ready for bed. He shared his frustrations about his limitations, and I helped him reframe

MY MOM AND DAD'S MESSAGE

..oughts by focusing on what he *could* do. We brainstormed about alternative ways to participate with the other campers so he didn't feel left out. For most of the activities, we found a way for him to join in, but there were some things he just couldn't do. Many of the nights, Gabe was discouraged and sad. I prayed with him, asking God to help us figure things out so he could get the most out of the camp.

One night after I sent him back to his cabin, the realization of what Gabe's abilities were compared to the other kids' was hitting me hard. I went to my cabin and cried myself to sleep. It was a very hard time for me, but I didn't want anyone to know I was struggling, especially Gabe. I simply stuffed my pain, put a smile on my face, and moved through the days.

Even with these disappointments, there were treasured moments of seeing God at work that entire week. Gabe felt close to God as he made new friends. At most meals, all the girls in my cabin asked him to eat at their table. And the camp counselors did a good job trying to accommodate our unique needs. I call these moments when I sense God at work "kisses on the cheek from God." These are reminders that He is with us, even in the hard times.

One of my favorite memories was when the worship team led the campers in a beautiful song that encouraged them to give their struggles to God and to "come just as you are." I watched Gabe get out of his wheelchair and walk to the front of the chapel. A group of new friends surrounded him with prayer as he set his discouragement on the altar before God. It was a sweet moment, and it felt a little bit like heaven to see these young people ministering to my brokenhearted son.

By the end of the week, Gabe sensed God's plan for him to share his story with other kids to encourage them in their own disappointments. Even as a young fifth-grade boy, he knew God would use his story to help others. Two years later, he started speaking in a school assembly program. God's plan was put into action.

MY MESSAGE IS C.L.E.A.R.

You can imagine the emotion that welled up in my heart as I sat in my room at Camp Berachah, all those years later, finalizing this book at the very place where God met Gabe and ministered to his broken heart. I took another walk around the campus and allowed God to minister to all the sadness I had stuffed so many years ago. I listened to worship music on my iPod and let the tears flow. It was such a sweet moment to see how God had taken us full circle in the process of laying our burdens at His feet. I'm thankful for the healing that took place in our lives. It is the picture of God's redemptive power to take life's disappointments and turn them into something good. It brings a true smile to my face.

My hope and prayer is that Gabe's story will help you to receive healing from whatever issues you face. One thing is very clear to me: God wants to heal your broken heart.

I'd love to help you process whatever grief you may experience in your journey through life. Please contact me on our website if you need encouragement.

Dad's Turn

I vividly remember the details of the day Gabe was born. Gigi and I were excited to meet our new baby. When the doctor announced that we had a boy and he had some problems, I wasn't sure if I should focus on Gabe or on helping Gigi. I ended up letting the doctor perform all the different tests on Gabe while I made sure Gigi was okay.

That evening was a blur of doctors and nurses making sure Gabe didn't have any life-threatening problems. We were thankful when they reported his major organs were healthy. Once I knew more about what was going on, I called the family to tell them that our son was born with major congenital birth defects. That was the hardest part. I didn't know how to tell them the difficult news. But everyone was very supportive and told us we'd all get through it together.

MY MOM AND DAD'S MESSAGE

Late that night, after things settled down, I went home and combed through my college anatomy books, trying to understand what was going on with Gabe's arm and leg bones. So many things were still unknown. I searched for understanding.

Gigi's mom was at our house watching Zane, and she and I talked long into the night. She helped me to process the shock of the situation. She listened to my concerns and encouraged me to take one day at a time.

I knew I had to stay strong and support my wife and sons, but honestly, I was terrified of what the future might hold for us. I knew if Gigi and I focused on what Gabe *could* do instead of what he *couldn't* do, we would be able to find a way to make the best of a difficult situation.

We took Gabe home two days after he was born. It was Easter Sunday. I was thankful that my parents were in town, and we spent time with both families. The activity was a great distraction from what we were facing. The love and support of our families helped me get through the early days of coming to grips with the reality of our future.

Over the next year, we discovered more about all of Gabe's issues. We had appointments with doctors at Children's Hospital and a University of Washington team that was part of the limb clinic. Some doctors suggested surgery, and others advised us to wait and see how Gabe developed.

The best advice we got from any of the doctors was from Dr. Teresa Massagli, who reminded us that we could do a variety of experimental surgeries or prosthetics to try to make Gabe's body more "normal," but the best thing we could do for him was to love him just the way he is. She encouraged us to treat him the same way we treated Zane. She said that love was the key to helping Gabe figure out how to live in his unusual body.

We took her advice and created an environment where Gabe could thrive. Zane was awesome with him, and together they grew up to be incredible young men who make this dad proud. I could not ask for a better family than my wife and two sons.

It took me about two years of struggling with the reality of our situation to get to a place of healing. Our good friend Diane Newman Holmstrom helped us to realize we could not deal with our issues on our own. She invited us to attend a Sunday service with her at Eastside Foursquare Church, where we found the hope and peace we needed to get through each day.

It is because of having Gabe in my life that I've grown to trust God with all of the issues we have faced. Over these last two decades, God has provided a way for our family to make the best of our situation. I am thankful for the strength we have found in knowing that God will make a way even when there does not seem to be one.

One thing I have done with Gabe is remove the word "can't" from his vocabulary. I help him find a way to do the things he'd like to do. We experiment and figure out what works. This has been a successful way to help him thrive.

When he wanted to try snowboarding, we told John at the Woodinville Ski Shop, and he bolted an apple crate to a snowboard. Gabe was a little top heavy, so we took a different approach. We found that he could ski on a bi-ski through the Outdoors for All program. It was fun to share my love of skiing with both of my sons.

We brainstormed ideas about how Gabe could participate in marching band and drive his wheelchair at the same time. I contacted our friend Jeff Jones. He let Gabe help him weld the bracket to hold his drum on his wheelchair. I wish you could have seen the smile on Gabe's face as he was driving his chair with his foot and pounding on his drum with his drumsticks in his hands. He loved performing with the rest of the Woodinville High School Marching Band. I'm so thankful that Eric Lucas let him participate in the band.

When Gabe kept scraping his knee on the gravel during baseball,

MY MOM AND DAD'S MESSAGE

I contacted Chick's Shoes in Mercer Island to ask if they could help design some sort of leather covering for his knee. Before long, they designed a perfect shoe to protect his left knee and shin as he hops around the bases. They also added a soft foam pad to his scooter to raise his knee off the pavement.

Participating in baseball with Gabe has been incredible. It was an avenue God provided for my healing. I really want to encourage you to share the Challenger Little League information with anyone who wants to have fun in a sport that serves every type of disability. This outlet has been a great way for Gabe and me to share our love for baseball and enjoy some father-son time. I highly recommend it for participants and spectators alike.

I am so proud of Gabe and the story that is unfolding as he continues to live out God's purpose for his life. I'm glad he has this opportunity to share it in a book. We hope it has been a helpful tool for you to see that no matter what circumstances you find yourself in, there is hope to get you through.

What the enemy meant for evil, God has helped us turn for good. Together we plan to help other families walk through the challenges of living with a disability in the most productive way. The idea of creating Gabriel's Foundation of HOPE was on my heart long before we ever took action. It is my passion to come alongside families and point them to hope.

Please take advantage of the resource section of this book as well as the information on our website. God bless you with hope and strength in the midst of life's greatest adversities.

MY MESSAGE IS C.L.E.A.R.

Gigi and Steve Murfitt, my mom and dad.

Our non-profit bought Kobey a new computer. He uses voice activated software to complete his homework.

CHAPTER 14

MY C.L.E.A.R. CHALLENGE TO YOU

WELL, HERE WE are at the end of my book. Thank you for taking the time to read about my life. I hope there is at least one thing you have taken away from reading my story and understanding my C.L.E.A.R. message.

I challenge you to live your life with Courage, Leadership, Endurance, Attitude, and Respect. Engage some of your friends in a challenge to live in such a way that you make a difference in someone else's life.

You have a future that is good. I just know it. Maybe right now you can't see it, but I hope my story will help turn your focus to the positive things in your situation. I hope I have made it C.L.E.A.R. that God loves you and has an amazing plan to use you to do something good.

I'd love to hear your story and encourage you in whatever you are going through. Find my page on Facebook®, or e-mail me at Gabe@ GabesHOPE.org. If you want to send me a note in the mail, please send it to:

Gabe Murfitt

Gabriel's Foundation of HOPE

PO Box 2437

Woodinville, WA 98072-2437

MY C.L.E.A.R. CHALLENGE TO YOU

At the end of this book, I've created a resource section to point you to some of the organizations that have helped me to live successfully. I encourage you to check them out. If you have a need and are not sure who to contact, please e-mail me, and I'll help you find the right resource.

I wish you a long and happy life. I'm glad we met on the pages of this book. I hope someday we'll get to meet in person. Keep in touch.

HELPFUL RESOURCES

Gabriel's Foundation of HOPE helps individuals and families dealing with disabilities to overcome and persevere through their challenges. Find information on grants and scholarships. HOPE stands for Help-Overcome-Persevere-Encourage. DONATE so we can help more people! For more information, write to:

Gabriel's Foundation of HOPE
PO Box 2437
Woodinville, WA 98072-2437
E-mail: Info@GabesHOPE.org
Website: http://www.GabesHOPE.org
Office phone: 425-483-0750 or 206-715-0134
President: Steve Murfitt

Joni and Friends is about advancing disability ministry and changing the church and communities around the world. The Joni and Friends International Disability Center (IDC) serves as the administrative center for ministries that provide outreach to thousands of families affected by disabilities around the globe.

Joni and Friends International Disability Center
PO Box 3333
Agoura Hills, CA 91376-3333
Website: http://www.joniandfriends.org

HELPFUL RESOURCES

Phone: 818-707-5664 Product Orders: 800-736-4177
Fax: 818-707-2391 TTY: 818-707-9707

Nick Vujicic—Life Without Limbs has a mission to cross boundaries and break down barriers, to build bridges that bring people to the love and hope found in Jesus Christ. Because Nick's unique personal story gives him favor with children, teens, and adults of any nationality and from various backgrounds, he is able to speak into the lives and hearts of many! His disability does not in any way diminish his ability to inspire others and spark the flame of hope in people's lives.

International Headquarters:
Life Without Limbs
PO Box 2430
Agoura Hills, CA 91376
Website: http://www.lifewithoutlimbs.org
Phone: 818-706-3300 Fax: 818-706-3363

DO-IT stands for Disability-Opportunity-Internetworking-Technology. The international DO-IT Center promotes the success of individuals with disabilities and the use of computer and networking technologies to increase their independence, productivity, and participation in education and careers. For more information write to:

DO-IT
University of Washington
Box 354842
Seattle, WA 98195-4842
E-mail: doit@uw.edu
Website: http://www.washington.edu/doit/
Phone: 206-685-DOIT (3648) (voice/TTY)
888-972-DOIT (3648) (toll free voice/TTY)

MY MESSAGE IS C.L.E.A.R.

(Fax) 206-221-4171
Spokane phone: 509-328-9331
Director: Sheryl Burgstahler, PhD

Department of Vocational Rehabilitation (DVR) believes employment contributes to a person's ability to live independently and that everyone has a right to work. Their purpose is to empower people with disabilities to achieve a greater quality of life by obtaining and maintaining employment. Search the web for the DVR office in your state.

Department of Vocational Rehabilitation
PO Box 45340
Olympia, WA 98504-5340
Website: http://www.dshs.wa.gov/dvr/
Phone: 360-725-3636 Toll Free: 800-637-5627

Department of Social and Health Services (DSHS) is an integrated organization of high-performing programs working in partnership for statewide impact to help transform lives. The department's mission is to improve the safety and health of individuals, families, and communities by providing leadership and establishing and participating in partnerships.

Department of Social and Health Services
Constituent Services
PO Box 45130
Olympia, WA 98504-5130
Website: http://www.dshs.wa.gov/
Phone: 800-737-0617

HELPFUL RESOURCES

Supplemental Security Income (SSI) pays benefits to disabled adults and children with limited income and resources. The Social Security Administration delivers services through a nationwide network of over 1,400 offices that include regional offices, field offices, card centers, teleservice centers, processing centers, hearing offices, the Appeals Council, and State and territorial partners (the Disability Determination Services). They also have a presence in US embassies around the globe. Contact your local office or write to:

Social Security Administration
Office of Public Inquiries
Windsor Park Building
6401 Security Blvd.
Baltimore, MD 21235
Website: http://www.ssa.gov/pgm/disability.htm
Phone: 800-772-1213

Aging and Disability Services Administration (ADSA) serves adults with chronic illnesses or conditions and people of all ages with developmental disabilities. All long-term care and Division of Developmental Disabilities (DDD) services are voluntary.

ADSA Headquarters
Blake Office Park West
4450 10th AVE SE Lacey, WA 98503
Website: http://www.adsa.dshs.wa.gov/
Toll Free 1-800-422-3263 TTY 1-877-905-0454

OUTDOORS for ALL has a mission to "enrich the quality of life for children and adults with disabilities through outdoor recreation." The Outdoors for All Foundation is a national leader and one of the largest nonprofit organizations providing year-round instruction in outdoor recreation for people with physical, developmental, and sensory disabilities. They have been assisting people since 1978.

MY MESSAGE IS C.L.E.A.R.

Outdoors for All Foundation
2 Nickerson Street, Suite 101
Seattle, WA 98109-1652
Phone: 206.838.6030
Fax: 206.838.6035
E-mail: Info@OutdoorsForAll.org
Website: http://www.outdoorsforall.org/

Challenger Division Little League was established in 1989 as a separate division of Little League to enable boys and girls with physical and mental challenges, ages four to eighteen, or up to age twenty-two if still enrolled in high school, to enjoy the game of baseball along with the millions of other children who participate in this sport worldwide. Today, more than thirty thousand children participate in more than nine hundred Challenger Divisions worldwide. The Seattle area coordinator is Bev Newsome. One of the coaches of the Woodinville Blue Jays is my dad, Steve Murfitt. E-mail us at info@GabesHOPE.org, and we'll get you connected with one of our local teams. It is a blast!

Website: http://www.littleleague.org/learn/about/divisions/
challenger.htm

RipkenCamps.com: Ripken Baseball instructional programs combine the wisdom of Cal Ripken, Sr. and his teachings with the thirty-three years of major league experience accumulated by both Cal Ripken, Jr. and Bill Ripken, creating memorable baseball experiences for young players and coaches alike. The Cal Ripken, Sr. Foundation does baseball- and softball-themed programs that help build character in and teach critical life lessons to disadvantaged young people living in America's most distressed communities.

Website: http://www.RipkenCamps.com

HELPFUL RESOURCES

Positive Programs Incorporated: Positive Programs Services, Inc. is a nonprofit organization providing nationally acclaimed, innovative assembly and concert programs to schools and educational/community organizations. Students love the relevant and entertaining programs. Faculty and parents appreciate the effectiveness of the presentations, as the professional performers and inspiring messages motivate every member of each audience to reach their dreams.

Positive Programs Incorporated
Director: Shari Rusch Furnstahl
PO Box 1628
Sumner, WA 98390
E-mail: ArcPress@comcast.net
Website: http://www.PositivePrograms.net
Office: 253-863-7672
Cell: 425-488-7672
Fax: 253-840-2030

MY MESSAGE IS C.L.E.A.R.

Speaking Engagements

To book Gabe Murfitt for speaking engagements, please contact us through http://www.GabesHOPE.org or send an e-mail to info@GabesHOPE.org. Donations to Gabriel's Foundation of HOPE provide the funds for Gabe to speak to schools at a minimal cost to the school. Businesses have often funded an assembly so that more students can hear this life-changing message. Please let us know if your business is interested in sponsoring a speaking event. Please call 206-715-0134 if you have questions.

To book Gigi Devine Murfitt for speaking engagements, please contact her through http://www.GigiMurfitt.com. You can also send an e-mail to Gigi@GigiMurfitt.com to request more information.

The Speakers Connection

Both Gigi and Gabe are part of the Speaker's Connection which is part of the Northwest Christian Writer's Association. Here is a link where you can get more information about booking speakers for your next event: www.nwchristianwriters.org.

OTHER BOOKS WRITTEN BY GIGI DEVINE MURFITT

Caregivers' Devotions to Go

Caregivers' Devotions to Go is for anyone with a heart to care for others. It speaks to young moms, grandmothers, adult children, and many others given the charge of caring for another person. It offers encouragement for a difficult task and gives both professional and

OTHER BOOKS WRITTEN BY GIGI DEVINE MURFITT

family caregivers a breath of fresh air to continue the assignment God has given them.

The Scripture verses and stories in this book encourage caregivers as they receive a blessing from the Lord for their servants' hearts. They also help caregivers know they are not alone in the task set before them and help the caregivers to see those in their care through the eyes of God—as fearfully and wonderfully made individuals.

The e-book version is available at http://www.Amazon.com. The printed book is available at http://www.GigiMurfitt.com.

If you wish to purchase more than one printed book, please e-mail Gigi at Gigi@GigiMurfitt.com

Thank you and God bless you for caring for others.

HOPE-FILLED SCRIPTURES

There are many Scriptures that have helped me clearly live a hope-filled life. For every new situation I face, I can always find hope by reading my Bible.

> Yet what we suffer now is nothing compared to the glory he will reveal to us later. For all creation is waiting eagerly for that future day when God will reveal who his children really are. Against its will, all creation was subjected to God's curse. But with eager hope, the creation looks forward to the day when it will join God's children in glorious freedom from death and decay. For we know that all creation has been groaning as in the pains of childbirth right up to the present time. And we believers also groan, even though we have the Holy Spirit within us as a foretaste of future glory, for we long for our bodies to be released from sin and suffering. We, too, wait with eager hope for the day when God will give us our full rights as his adopted children, including the new bodies he has promised us. We were given this hope when we were saved. (If we already have something, we don't need to hope for it. But if we look forward to something we don't yet have, we must wait patiently and confidently.)
>
> —Romans 8:18–25 NLT

> May the God of hope fill you with all joy and peace as you trust in him, so that you may overflow with hope by the power of the Holy Spirit.
>
> —Romans 15:13

HOPE-FILLED SCRIPTURES

For You are my hope, O Lord GOD; You are my trust from my youth. By You I have been upheld from birth; you are He who took me out of my mother's womb. My praise shall be continually of You.

—Psalm 71:5–6

For everything that was written in the past was written to teach us, so that through the endurance taught in the Scriptures and the encouragement they provide we might have hope. May the God who gives endurance and encouragement give you the same attitude of mind toward each other that Christ Jesus had, so that with one mind and one voice you may glorify the God and Father of our Lord Jesus Christ.

—Romans 15:4–6

We use the Internet to search the Bible for helpful verses for whatever we are going through. Check out this helpful website: http://www.BibleGateWay.com. Use the "Keyword Search" button to find specific words all throughout Scripture. It will help you to live a C.L.E.A.R. life.

ENDNOTES

1. http://dictionary.reference.com/browse/courage
2. The *Seattle Times* Archives http://community.seattletimes.nwsource.com/archive/?date=20030413&slug=gabe13e
3. http://dictionary.reference.com/browse/leadership
4. http://en.wikipedia.org/wiki/Leadership
5. http://dictionary.reference.com/browse/endurance
6. Henry Ford. BrainyQuote.com, Xplore Inc, 2011. http://www.brainyquote.com/quotes/authors/h/henry_ford_2.html, accessed December 5, 2011.
7. http://dictionary.reference.com/browse/attitude
8. John Maxwell, *The 21 Irrefutable Laws of Leadership*, Thomas Nelson Publishing, 1998 and 2007
9. http://dictionary.reference.com/browse/respect
10. http://www.searchquotes.com/quotation/Respect_for_the_fragility_and_importance_of_an_individual_life_is_still_the_mark_of_an_educated_man./33414/
11. http://dictionary.reference.com/browse/hope
12. http://thinkexist.com/quotation/learn_from_yesterday-live_for_today-hope_for/222120.html
13. http://thinkexist.com/quotation/optimism_is_the_faith_that_leads_to_achievement/13582.html
14. http://dictionary.reference.com/browse/help

ENDNOTES

15. http://dictionary.reference.com/browse/overcome
16. http://dictionary.reference.com/browse/persevere
17. http://dictionary.reference.com/browse/encourage

Gabriel's Foundation of HOPE

Bringing HOPE to the world

Thank you for purchasing this book.
A portion of the sale of each book helps Gabriel's
Foundation of HOPE reach families in need.
Visit our website for more information about our
nonprofit organization.
E-mail: Info@GabesHOPE.org
Website: http://www.GabesHOPE.org
Office phone: 425-483-0750 or 206-715-0134